THE BIBLE IN A WORLD CONTEXT

THE BIBLE IN A WORLD CONTEXT

*An Experiment in
Contextual Hermeneutics*

Edited by

Walter Dietrich *&* Ulrich Luz

WILLIAM B. EERDMANS PUBLISHING COMPANY
GRAND RAPIDS, MICHIGAN / CAMBRIDGE, U.K.

Wm. B. Eerdmans Publishing Co.
255 Jefferson Ave. S.E., Grand Rapids, Michigan 49503 /
P.O. Box 163, Cambridge CB3 9PU U.K.

Printed in the United States of America

07 06 05 04 03 02   7 6 5 4 3 2 1

Library of Congress Cataloging-in-Publication Data

The Bible in a world context: an experiment in contextual hermeneutics /
edited by Walter Dietrich & Ulrich Luz.
     p.   cm.
Includes bibliographical references.
ISBN 0-8028-4988-1 (pbk.: alk. paper)
1. Bible — Hermeneutics.   I. Dietrich, Walter.   II. Luz, Ulrich.

BS476.B493   2002
220.6'01 — dc21
                                       2001058457

www.eerdmans.com

CONTENTS

Preface   vii

THREE PROGRAMMATIC STUDIES
IN CONTEXTUAL HERMENEUTICS

Reading the Bible under a Sky without Stars   3

    Elsa Tamez

Inculturation Hermeneutics:
An African Approach to Biblical Interpretation   17

    Justin Ukpong

Ego and Self in the New Testament and in Zen   33

    Seiichi Yagi

IN THOSE DAYS A DECREE WAS
ISSUED BY THE EMPEROR AUGUSTUS . . . :
THREE CONTEXTUAL BIBLE STUDIES ON LUKE 2

A Star Illuminates the Darkness   53

    Elsa Tamez

CONTENTS

The Story of Jesus' Birth (Luke 1–2): An African Reading   59
  Justin Ukpong

Mary and Maya   71
  Seiichi Yagi

Instead of a Conclusion: Theological Astronomy — a Parable   77
  Walter Dietrich

PREFACE

At times, interpretations matter. On the whole, such times are
times of cultural crisis. The older ways of understanding and
practice, even experience itself, no longer seem to work. . . .
Then we need to reflect on what it means to interpret.[1]

This is how David Tracy put it. When he chose this formulation he might
have had Luther's Reformation discovery in mind. What he says is valid
for our present-day situation, too. In our own northern and western European context we experience especially that "the older ways of understanding" the Bible "no longer seem to work." The Protestant northern
and western Europe was shaped by the Bible. More than in any other area
of the world the Bible was *the* "book of books" for us. It was *the* foundation of truth, *the* source of individual piety. It was the starting point of
the European liberation movement, the foundation of morals, the basis
for political legitimization, and so on. That is no longer what the Bible is
today. Nowadays the Bible is less read in northern and western Europe
than in most other parts of the world, although it can be found everywhere indeed: standing on the shelves in everybody's home as a relic from
studying the subject "Religion" in school, or as a memory of one's wed-
ding ceremony in church. But it is covered in dust and long forgotten.

1. D. Tracy, *Plurality and Ambiguity: Hermeneutics, Religion, Hope* (San Francisco: Harper & Row, 1987), 7.

This is not the same in the Catholic parts of southern Europe: one of the lasting consequences of the *aggiornamento* starting with the Second Vatican Council has been the rediscovery of the Bible in the Roman Catholic Church. The status of the Bible is different, again, in the Orthodox, former communist parts of eastern Europe, where it is being rediscovered in these present days of radical changes and reorientation. In addition, its status is different in North America: time and again, it is amazing for us northern and western Europeans to see how little secularized the United States is, compared with our own countries. It is astonishing to realize that the Bible is a book that is alive and effective not only in fundamentalist or evangelical circles, but also within the mainstream churches. Where do these differences between North America and western Europe come from? We can imagine the reasons, but this is not the time and place to follow this up.

We encounter an altogether different situation in the African and South American countries. Here the Bible is an immeasurably valuable and powerful book, and countless people read it and listen to it. It is read and discussed mainly by groups and communities. David Tracy's thesis that in times of cultural crisis "interpretations matter" applies to Africa and South America: the people there read the Bible — torn between capitalism and extreme poverty, between individual, indigenous cultural roots and imported Western culture and science, fascinated by the never-ending task of adopting the Christian faith, which became homeless in western and northern Europe. For them, it was a new, alien faith, and they turned it into their own. Through their Bible reading they communicate with each other and draw their common identity from the Bible. The ordinary people who read the Bible like this are joined by Bible scholars: "reading with . . ." is a source of their hermeneutics; the "academy of the poor" becomes the place where they learn.[2] The South American and African biblical scholars are often torn between the standards set by the Western science of Bible exegesis,

2. Cf. the paper of J. S. Ukpong in this volume, 17-32; and G. O. West, *The Academy of the Poor: Towards a Dialogical Reading of the Bible* (Sheffield: Sheffield Academic Press, 1999).

which they want to take seriously, and their own contextual situation. Only because of their contextual situation are there a meaning and a value in the way they read the Bible, in their research and in their hermeneutical efforts.

Finally, the status of the Bible is different, again, in Asia. No country is similar to the other here, but the overall statement applies to many situations and to many countries: the Bible is read intensively. Let us take, for example, Japan, the richest and in some sense probably the most westernized Asian country. The Bible is read among the intellectuals of Japan more intensely than in the educated classes of western Europe, despite the fact that the majority do not belong to any church. Why? This, too, probably has to do with a cultural crisis in which Japan continuously finds itself, and which makes the reading of the Bible both necessary and fruitful. It is the tension between Western culture and their own Japanese roots. The fundamental conviction of the uniqueness and importance of the individual belongs to Western culture. To the Japanese roots belongs the conviction that not only in society the collective and the community is placed before the individual, but that also in religion the individual self can be understood only in relation to a transindividual ground, no matter whether it is called "Buddha," "God," or "Void." In this tension it is essential to search for one's own identity; and for that, again, reading the Bible is crucial, because the Bible is at the same time a main root of Western individualism and a common property of humankind in general.

When our own ways of understanding no longer work, it is essential to listen to others and learn from them. It seems to us that Western biblical scholarship suffers most from being "without context." It is carried out abstractly and therefore leads to abstract results and truths, which are not related to any context. "Abstract" is not only understood in the usual sense as being opposed to "concrete." "Abstract" also means: unattached to the life and reading of "ordinary" people, far away from their questions, developed in the ivory tower of the university. "Abstract" means: detached from the present and from its problems, concerned only with the reconstruction of a past with all its problems. Finally, another way of scholarly, "abstract" reading that is disconnected from the real concerns of present-day readers is to flee into an imaginary "text world" — imaginary, because it is entirely created by scholars. "Abstract" in the widest sense means: without context. All this does not contribute to understanding, which is related to our own context.

Because of this, it is *contextual* Bible reading and *contextual* Bible hermeneutics that we need most. Hermeneutics, which reflects understanding, is of importance for all the different disciplines that we call "humanities," actually, for every human being. It asks for the conditions of the understanding of other realities. Thereby it has to include the basic anthropological fact that every conception of reality leads to an act of interpretation. The other is always perceived from a given background and necessarily has to be imprinted on this life's horizon if profound understanding is to be achieved. If we think about perception of texts, one has to take into account that here, too, other realities are perceived and interpreted. Therefore, interpretation of all texts, biblical or other, always happens in both contexts: the past and the present. To a large extent, however, Western biblical scholarship is not aware of this.

Something else can be added in connection with the Bible. This book already adapted itself to very different cultural contexts even before we tried to understand it. In itself, the Bible combines many cultural horizons, from ancient Egypt to imperial Rome. It became the basic document of two world religions and together with them advanced from the narrow Palestinian world into the wide Hellenistic and Roman world. As Christianity and Judaism spread, the Bible reached the remotest ends of the world and influenced many cultures, which in turn understood and adopted it extremely differently. It did not hinder but rather advanced the emergence of various tendencies, movements, and denominations within the religions that had the Bible as their basis. Exceeding this basis, it had an effect on many other religions and also on irreligious contexts. To ask about the effect and fates of the biblical traditions in all these processes, about the conditions of understanding, and about the ways of the biblical texts in a multitude of cultural and religious contexts, and finally to ask about the particular emphasis in our own context: this is the task of contextual Bible hermeneutics.

Considering the lack of context that prevails to a large extent in our Western Bible research and taking into consideration that in other continents the particular contexts are much more evident and apparently affect very fruitfully Bible reading and Bible scholarship, we need impulses for contextual Bible hermeneutics from Asia, Africa, and Latin America. For us Bernese biblical scholars a surprising possibility arose to put this to the test. The Hans-Sigrist Foundation, named after a Bernese lawyer who left part of his wealth for the support of the sciences in Bern, announces, besides stipends, an annual well-paid prize for excellent, innovative, and promising scientific accomplishments. The area in which the prize is awarded is different every year and chosen by the board of the foundation. In the year 2000 the board decided to award the prize in the area of "contextual Bible hermeneutics," as was proposed by the Protestant Theological Faculty of the university.

All involved agreed that in order to find a prizeworthy accomplishment in this area one should deliberately turn to non-European contexts. This was the reason why the selection committee turned its attention right from the beginning to researchers in Africa, Latin America, and Asia who were worthy of the prize. The committee, which contained members of our faculty and some scholars from other universities, carried out a broad and worldwide consultation. As a result, they came up with a list of twenty-eight candidates, seven of whom were put on the short list after a careful evaluation. These were two black Africans, one white African, two Asians, and two Latin Americans. On the basis of the votes of six internationally acknowledged experts, the selection committee and in turn the board of the foundation finally decided on awarding the prize to Elsa Tamez from Costa Rica.

Some of the scholars whose names were discussed by the selection committee were not a possible choice for the Hans-Sigrist Prize out of purely external factors, such as age. Among those scholars whose names were discussed very intensely, two were very important: Seiichi Yagi from Japan and Justin Ukpong from Nigeria. The former is a New Testament and religious philosophy scholar, whose many books try to interpret the New Testament in the light of Buddhist thinking and thereby try to help Buddhists and Christians to discover themselves in the other and the other in themselves. The latter is a Catholic New Testament scholar whose attempts to read the Bible together with and for "ordinary people" are impressive. By doing so he wants to devote his Bible interpretations to the cause of creating an identity for and liberating the people in his home country. At the request of the selection committee the Protestant Theological Faculty of Bern decided to confer its honorary doctorate on Seiichi Yagi and Justin Ukpong.

On the occasion of awarding the Hans-Sigrist Prize and the honorary doctorates, a public symposium "The Bible in the World Context" was held. The papers published in this volume were presented at this occasion. Besides a basic paper, the three guests were also asked to give a Bible study on a text that was the same for all three speakers. When we chose the text, which relates, of course, more closely to some contexts than to others, we were guided by the season. The symposium was held shortly before Christmas of the year 2000, and we therefore found it suitable to choose the well-known Christmas story from Luke's Gospel.

For the realization of this publication we would like to thank: the Hans Sigrist Foundation, who not only awarded Mrs. Tamez the prize, but also financed the symposium and contributed toward the costs for the translation and the printing of this booklet; Mrs. Claudia Einsele-Egerer, student at the Theological Faculty of Bern, who helped in the careful process of the selection of the prizewinner and the preparation and implementation of the symposium. We extend our gratitude to the translators: Gloria Kinsler (San Salvador) translated the texts of Elsa Tamez from Spanish to English. Margun Welskopf (Bern) translated the texts of Seiichi Yagi and the texts of the editors from German into English; Stefan Dietrich translated the main papers of Elsa Tamez and Justin Ukpong into German. Finally we want to thank W. B. Eerdmans Publishing Co., particularly Mr. Sam Eerdmans, as well as the Theologischer Verlag Zürich and its director Dr. Niklaus Peter, who were willing to publish this volume in two different contexts and languages.

WALTER DIETRICH & ULRICH LUZ

THREE PROGRAMMATIC STUDIES
IN CONTEXTUAL HERMENEUTICS

READING THE BIBLE UNDER
A SKY WITHOUT STARS

Elsa Tamez

Abundance and Absence (Inmensidad y ausencia)

Canek, the Mayan sage, said to Guy, a fragile and noble child of the
plantation:
"Look at the sky; count the stars."
"It is not possible to count them."
Canek spoke to him again:
"Look at the earth; count the grains of sand."
"It is not possible to count them."
Canek then said:
"Even though it is not known, there exists a number for the stars
and a number for the grains of sand. But that which exists and cannot be counted and is felt here within requires a word to say it. The
word in this case would be 'abundance.' It is a word moist with mystery. This word makes it unnecessary to count the stars or the grains
of sand. We have traded *knowledge* for *emotion,* which is also a way to
penetrate into the truth of things."[1]

The wisdom of Canek introduces us to a new way of looking at
things, different from the way we are accustomed to look at things.

1. Ermilo Abreu Gómez, *Canek. Historia y leyenda de un heroe maya,* 33rd ed.
(Mexico, D.F.: Oaxis, 1977), 53-54; cf. the English translation: *Canek: History and Leg-
end of a Maya Hero* (Berkeley: University of California Press, 1979), 20.

There are things that exist; we are certain of that because we see them, like the stars, or we can touch them, like grains of sand. Although we cannot count them, they do not cease to exist because we cannot apply mathematics to them. They are there, and their presence demands a word to express, in this case, their number. We are dealing with words that include reason and sentiment. "Abundance" is one of these words. When I pronounce "abundance" I feel something in my breast, an emotion. Canek says that they are "words moist with mystery." They are moist with mystery because they do not exist alone and cannot be counted, but are felt, "here within." To see the sky overflowing with stars causes a profound emotion that is felt in one's breast. There is a relation of inexplicable complicity between the word *abundance* and the act of contemplating a black sky covered with stars. Because we tremble, it is our body and not our head that knows of this complicity. There are times and spaces where there is no room for arithmetic because the head unites with the heart and sabotages reason. Canek and Guy are this type of person; they see beyond things and penetrate their truth by different paths.

I think that these "words moist with mystery" are a different type. Sometimes emotions place themselves above words. For example, *abundance* is a word that evokes feelings of satisfaction and joyfulness when contemplating a starry sky. Now then, if there are no stars in the sky, the word *abundant* does not serve us, even though we know that the stars exist and are uncountable. This is because we have another feeling, a feeling that puts aside the reasoning of what is countable or uncountable. When we know that things exist but are not visible, counted or not, and we feel a lack "here within," the word *absence* would be the "word moist with mystery" that best expresses this reality of things. "Absence," as opposed to fullness or satisfaction, generates pain.

Today in Latin America we are living under a sky without stars. "Absence," with its list of synonyms — lack, privation, omission, estrangement, separation, departure, abandonment, exclusion, withdrawal, desertion — seems to me to be the word to define this reality. I am referring to the macrolevel, because when we look at the everyday level or at excluded groups such as indigenous peoples, African Latin

Americans, and women, we can distinguish lights in the night. But the sky that covers the continent and the Caribbean cries out "absence": absence of bread, love, justice, solidarity, movement, peace, of utopias, of God. The globalization of the economy, with its free market policies, is not only deepening the social divisions against which we struggled in the past decades, but also robbing us of the feelings that remind us of our humanity: to be moved when we are faced with the pain of our neighbor and our habitat. The birth and deepening of the absence come within the global framework that insists on delegitimizing any divergent proposal.

There were absences in past decades as well, of bread, work, peace, but the sky was completely illuminated. There was no Absence with a capital letter, nor was it felt — the absence of utopias or absence of God. The feeling of "abundance" lived in our hearts and gave us strength for the struggle against the injustices. Today we experience Absence, with a capital letter. The darkness of the sky without stars scatters us and forces us to withdraw into individualism. It is as if we were under a curfew; we stay inside our houses. We are in a crisis of paradigms, we are told, and the paradigm of capitalism grows stronger and stronger. To speak of revolution, organization, or consciousness raising is anachronistic, they tell us. And the dead in Colombia because of the war, and in the rest of the countries because of poverty, continue to increase. To speak of the historical actor is obsolete, and the indigenous peoples, African Latin Americans, and women who have become protagonists feel betrayed. They tell us that we have to be realistic, that there are no alternatives except in today's neoliberal policy. So the horizons continue close under a sky without stars. There are more and more street children, unemployment increases, the number of beaten and murdered women continues to rise, diseases eradicated years ago reappear, and strange new ones continue appearing. We are in a process of turning in upon ourselves, where reason loses ground in the face of irrationality. The politicians and philosophers go one way and realities go another way. And the people, agitated and crowded, run in search of the best religious offer that at least feeds their soul and helps them to withstand their poverty.

5

The 90s were definitely an era different from the 80s. In spite of a reality in which poverty exceeds that of the past decades, the spiritual strength of the struggle, the certainty of the possibility of change in society, has been absent. This is the reason that eyes have turned to the struggle of women, indigenous peoples, and African Latin Americans, who paradoxically, thanks to the silence of unions and leftist political organizations, have raised their voices, their own voices, with new tonalities and shades, to help recompose Latin American prophetical thinking.

This is the context in which we interpret the Bible in Latin America. Biblical scholarship alone is not sufficient to deal with the abundance or absence that we experience. In our hermeneutics there are passion and compassion, two human dimensions marginalized by the academy. But they are also ways to penetrate into the truth of things. They are words that are "moist with mystery," that by their magical art warm hearts — and heads — providing energy in the struggle for a dignified life for all men and women.

Your Word Is a Lamp to My Feet and a Light to My Path (Ps 119:105)

I believe that the most important and difficult task for Christians and those who want to have a relevant word for our current reality is to search for stars in the four cardinal points. Search for them in the house, in the street, in institutions and organizations, within oneself, and in the other. They have to be there. Search for them, even in impossible places: in the profound blackness of the sky, or in the depths of the sea, or maybe by digging deep into the earth, the stars will appear. We need more light and much wisdom to counteract the great Absence.

But to search for lights in the dark night we need a lantern that will light our feet and the path. For Christians, one of these lamps is the Bible.

What is the Bible? For many of us in Latin America the Bible is a mysterious book, good and cruel at the same time. It can promote peace as well as violence. In it we find abundance and absence, as we do in our realities. It cannot be any other way. The Bible narrates diverse worlds in their own times, realities like ours, although ancient and complex to our understanding. In these worlds of the Bible we find beautiful utopias, as well as texts of terror, and we confront a God who is merciful and just, and sometimes not so merciful or just. This is what is so fascinating about the Bible: that our life, equally complex and ambiguous, is seen reflected in this book.

The variety of worlds that the diverse texts show and their polysemy, of course, invite multiple entrance ways to search for that lantern that will illuminate some of the path that is ours to walk today, because not all the Bible is a lantern, nor is it all darkness. Neither do the lanterns always serve as lanterns, nor the darkness as darkness. Sometimes, in a particular context, a lantern-text no longer gives light, and a darkness-text is changed into light. It all depends on the context in which it is read. A text is entered intentionally to search for the lights that serve as criteria for illuminating our thought, attitude, and practice. For that reason, Latin American biblical hermeneutics, in the last instance, is nothing but an intentional digging for hope in the texts, for the poor and excluded: a word of encouragement, dignity, solidarity, and strength.

In the Bible some texts always remain as lanterns, for example: God is love, God defends the poor. And some texts of terror are unlikely to give light. What do we do with these? This is the problem that often arises for those of us who recognize the Bible as the canon of the written Word. Sometimes they are ignored and are left there as a witness to negativity. It cannot be "the will of God" that women are killed, and violence is unleashed between tribes, as in Judges 19–21. Nor can genocide, because of the resistance of others to submit to the God championed by the conquerors, be "the will of God."

At other times — more frequently today — we work these texts with all the possible methods at hand that might help to explain them. And, if it is impossible to find light for today's practices, we set them aside on a second level.

Intentional selection is one of the characteristics of contextual

7

biblical hermeneutics, precisely because we begin with our context and the context orients the exegete or the common reader to choose those texts that are a lamp to the feet and a light for the path. Manipulation? Antiscientific? No. It is the desperate need to grasp onto a light for a particular situation.

Life: A Mantle of Stars

Even though the stars are thousands of light years away — according to the scientists — and the clouds swallow up their splendor, we feel them "here within." If our people and diverse communities have resisted for so many years poverty, pain, and repression, it is because of the light they carry within them. It is sometimes vigorous and sometimes weak, but it is inextinguishable. Not because of a special gift given to the people of Latin America, but because it is an inherent quality of the human being: to live joyously, to struggle for life, and to defend it.

For many years, first at the point of a sword and later with bullets, alienating religious and political discourse were used to try to impose resignation, but that has not been possible. The light of life, received as a gift from God and a human right, has not allowed that to happen. Today they want to impose resignation by the decree of free market laws, but it will be impossible. We can live under a sky without stars, but not without the stars that shine in our daily struggle. Because, when the stars are extinguished within us, life ends. Our stars are like the Holy Spirit: they give witness that the starry sky exists, that it evokes abundance, in spite of the fact that the clouds persist in casting Absence.

In his inauguration speech as president of South Africa, Nelson Mandela said, "We are born to manifest the glory of God that is within us. It is not only in some chosen ones: it is in each one of us, and in the measure we let our own light shine, without knowing it, we let others do the same" (1994).

Some might say to us, What, concretely, is this Absence? Here I could enumerate the statistics from the United Nations on the economic situation of poor, less poor, and rich countries. Statistics for how many children die of hunger, or adults who do not reach forty years of age, which is the average for Haiti, and the many deaths that take place daily in Colombia. But official facts demonstrate little, hardly enough to show the reality and feeling of Absence. In truth, the situation of misery and death cannot be counted, as we cannot count the stars or the grains of sand on the earth. The percentage of unemployed, or the deaths because of war, show only a number. Behind each number there is a tragedy, due to that unemployment or death, known only to the family and the neighbors.

Neither can we enumerate the statistics of the reactions of different movements against the Absence. Even though this decade is darker, we see light when we hear of protests in Peru, when the indigenous peoples, women, and African Latin Americans meet, denounce, and contribute to the clearing of the horizon by making new proposals of light.

In Latin American biblical hermeneutics, real life, corporal and sensual, lived in different concrete contexts, is the starting point for biblical analysis. Here we also find lights, lamps that take us to the Bible and illuminate texts that at the same time are changed into lamps. There occurs a mutual illumination. The life-light shines and kindles the light of the text and this in turn illuminates life, showing usable meanings, be it to resist, to understand, or to transform painful realities.

Partiality for the Excluded

Conscious partiality is a characteristic of Latin American hermeneutics. When we look for lights to illuminate a miserable present, objectivity is impossible. Because on the imperfect and conflictive frontiers of human history, there are always those who become victims of a system that tends to organize things according to who has power. This is a problem in all systems. Latin America is a poor continent that revolves around Western civilization; therefore, the relations of globalized power appear on this continent. The Mexican *rancheros*, the Colombian *cumbias*, the Brazilian *samba*, and the flutes of the Andes will distinguish them from other continents, but their logos, which are "borrowed," and the relations of power will be the same. Those who benefit from the system are the wealthy, whites, and men, with their respective tenor. Those most prejudiced against are the poor, those with black or dark skin, indigenous peoples, African Latin Americans, and women. Other excluded persons who do not fit into the patterns of the capitalist, patriarchal society are sexual minorities, the differently abled, the elderly, and children.

Certainly, partiality for the excluded in Latin American hermeneutics is inevitable if we want to be just and credible. The academy will have to put itself at the service of life for all people. There is no way to do that except from the locus of the excluded, whether because of race or gender. From this locus, biblical interpretation can contribute, explicitly or implicitly, to a society where there is room for all men and women. This would be a great light on the horizon, an organizing principle of hope.[2]

New Lights in the Dark Night

We have spoken of Absence with a capital letter, as that word "moist with mystery" that reflects the nonpresence of our longings at the macrolevel. The terrorizing statistics of violence and death, malnutrition and illiteracy, poverty and unemployment shed light on the Absence, hidden sometimes by the fascination of economic growth and technological advances in communications. Nevertheless, we find here and there, even under the great sky without lights, "constellations" of stars with the faces of women, indigenous peoples, or African Latin Americans. And these constellations are illuminating the Bible and life with new lights, lights of different colors and forms unknown until now. The Bible, a book that has been read with the same eyes for so many years, is undergoing an upheaval when read by women, indige-

2. Terms used in the Community of Ecumenical Theological Education in Latin America and the Caribbean, CETELA Congress in Medellin, Colombia, 1997.

nous peoples, or African Latin Americans. It is here that race, class, and gender interweave. When we apply other hermeneutics to the Bible, things come to light that are unsuspected, good, and challenging. It is these new insights that are igniting lights in the Bible that were hidden before.

Latin American hermeneutics is becoming more consolidated all the time. It deals with a feminist hermeneutic that confronts the text as patriarchal, and repudiates interpretations that are harmful to women. Within these tasks, it explores new methods to illuminate the forced silence to which women were submitted in biblical times by the authors, who produced an androcentric text. This Latin American hermeneutics is allied with other feminist exegetes from other continents — sharing their methods but without leaving behind the situation of the great Absence — that challenge and judge in favor of life for all.

Indigenous hermeneutics, strengthened by the reminder of five centuries and now hit hard by official documents of ecclesiastical control,[3] shows how a constellation can share lights with other non-Christian constellations. Biblical interpretation, from this cultural angle, is generating new meanings that have helped to illuminate the grassroots reading of the Bible. Its syncretistic newness provokes, of course, a reaction from those who have been formed in Christian orthodoxy. But the challenges presented and the questions generated will help to enrich the intentions of Christianity itself. I would hope that ears will not be closed to this new cry from a culture that is demanding its place, with an ancient spirituality in a continent that marginalizes them.

The African Latin American hermeneutic is a challenging light that speaks to all hermeneutics and alerts them against racism present in all groups of society. Its light illuminates the hidden racism that appears, many times in an unconscious way, camouflaged or even unnoticed. From this hermeneutic we learn to rescue the memory of the African Latin Americans from their past enslavement and come to appreciate their resistance to the suffering and humiliation of which

---

3. Cardinal Ratzinger's document "Dominus Iesus" is a frontal attack on this hermeneutic.

they were victims. Even more, this hermeneutic is able to reappropriate the liberating message of the Judeo-Christian Scriptures, in spite of the fact that they were frequently used to legitimize slavery.

These new constellations are new lights that illuminate everyday life and social life under a sky without stars. They remind us that the stars are there, in the profundity of the universe, although we can not see them for now. . . .

The Search for Stars at Different Levels

When we in Latin America speak of hermeneutics, we have to distinguish different levels. The Bible has been one of the most studied books during the 80s and 90s in both the Catholic and Protestant churches. The levels of hermeneutics are important because in biblical research we need to pay attention to the production of meaning that is being done in the grassroots communities. Although their contribution is at the level of intuition, biblical scholars have to receive the creativity that comes from there and then take it to the text for rigorous study.

We distinguish three hermeneutical levels: the academic level, a middle level, and the grassroots level. The research or academic level is that of professional biblical scholars. This level works with the text in the original languages and uses exegetical methods, the study of contexts within the cultural, political, and economic realities of the periods in which the texts were written. At this level the research is usually written.

The middle level is that of pastoral agents who are trained in workshops for biblical education. These have a certain academic rigor and seek to circulate the study of the Bible to a wide sector at the grassroots level. This level can also be written, in a simpler style, but it can also be spoken, poetic, and very creative.

The grassroots level corresponds to the ecclesial communities who by themselves, or with the guidance of a biblical advisor or a pastoral agent, rediscover the biblical meanings. Maybe here we cannot speak of biblical research in the strictest sense; nevertheless, meaning is produced at the level of intuition. At this level the work is generally oral and uses narrative, poetry, or song.

The interrelation among these levels is constant. Most of the professional biblical scholars I know work with grassroots communities. The majority are able to move within the distinct levels, whether oral or written. Poetic creativity can appear at all levels, not just at the grassroots. The study done at these levels can be seen in the bibliographical database that is produced in Brazil.[4] Occasionally, there are tensions between the levels. Some are criticized by scholars and others by the grassroots sectors. There is, however, a consensus about the necessity of articulating between the levels, because the final goal of biblical research is to give meaning and dignity to the lives of persons and communities.

Therefore, to continue with the metaphor of light, on the different levels of biblical interpretation we find a concert of fireflies, that, together from their specific tasks, illuminate the text in the search for liberating meanings.

Paths in Search of Stars

In order to find lights in the Bible, Latin American biblical scholars take different paths. There is no one privileged method. The major concern and contribution of the Latin American biblical approach are in contextual hermeneutics, not in exegesis itself. But without good exegesis, the hermeneutics will be poor. That is why we try to work with the texts rigorously, using those methods that the text itself calls for, in order to show more clearly its meanings of solidarity with the excluded. The exegetical methods vary, depending on the scholar and his or her education. The exegeses most used are sociological, historical, economic, semiotic, structuralist, and more recently reception criticism. The methods of higher criticism are used when the information is useful for hermeneutics in the production of meaning and not as an aca-

---

4. Cf. *Bibliografia Biblica Latino America* (Pétropolis, Brasil: EMESP, Vozes).

demic requirement. We appreciate the research done by First World biblical scholars, especially those who help in the understanding of the socioeconomic, cultural, and theological contexts of the production of the text.[5]

The Walk until Now

Reading the Bible under "a sky without stars" shows the difficulty we experience when faced with the great Absence. Nevertheless, we do not place ourselves on the side of pessimism because of that difficulty. When we speak about reading the Bible in this context, we throw ourselves into the search for light, with a firm faith of finding in the Word that which according to the psalmists is a lamp and a light. The Absence is the presence of that which is absent, that which we desire (a life of dignity for all men and women),[6] and for that reason, it passes judgment on the present and calls for action.

Because contextual biblical hermeneutics is questioned by this Absence, in Latin America we can speak of a biblical movement that is well organized throughout the continent. In fact, the study of the Bible in Latin America has been one of the most stimulating and fascinating areas during the 80s and 90s. Concretely, there is the network of grassroots Bible reading established some years ago; the Intensive Bible Course (CIB) takes place in various countries and consists of six months of intensive preparation for pastoral agents in which well-known Bible scholars participate as advisors;[7] and the annual meetings

5. This includes Richard Horsley, Elisabeth Schüssler-Fiorenza, Gerd Theissen, Bruce M. Malina, Wayne M. Meeks, John P. Meier, John H. Elliott, Sean Freyne, and many others.

6. The theme of Absence as a presence of absence is a theme that was discussed by the Departmento Ecumenico de Investigaciones (DEI) in the last seminar of invited researchers, August-November, 2000.

7. Among them, Milton Schwantes, Carlos Mesters, José Severino Croatto, Pablo Richard, Jorge Pixley, Tania Mara Sampaio, Nancy Cardoso, Irene Foulkes, Nestor Miguez, Silvia de Lima, myself, and others.

of Latin American Bible scholars to prepare the *RIBLA* magazine are among the most stimulating events. Beside these, in the last two years a group of women biblical scholars has formed with the intention of supporting the study of the Bible from the perspective of gender. The diversity of themes approached, always challenged by real and concrete life, and the plurality of methods used, make the meanings produced in the text rich and pertinent.

Abundance within the Absence

The Mayan sage Canek applies the emotions felt in the counting of the stars as a valid way to know the truth of things. "Abundance," he says, is the word required when confronted with the impossibility of counting the stars in a night covered with them. Today, when we look for lights to illuminate our paths under a sky without stars that evokes Absence, and we find them and share them, and when we see the network of the Bible movement and biblical scholars supporting with their lights, it is impossible to count the fireflies that participate in the search for stars. So, like Canek, we have to pronounce the "word moist with mystery" that causes satisfaction within: "abundance." I conclude by saying that, even though it seems paradoxical, it is possible to speak of "abundance" in the midst of Absence.

INCULTURATION HERMENEUTICS:
AN AFRICAN APPROACH TO
BIBLICAL INTERPRETATION

Justin Ukpong

Introduction

In academic readings of the Bible in Africa, the Western and the specifically African methods of reading exist side by side. For want of a better term and in contradistinction to the African ways of reading, I designate classical Western Bible reading methodologies as *intellectualist*. By that I mean that they professedly seek objective truth as interpretive interest, and profess to employ a universal perspective. A major concern is knowledge of the meaning of the biblical text through the use of methods of investigation established and acknowledged as critical by the academy. Their conclusions are expected to have a universal application. By contrast, however, African readings are *existential and pragmatic* in nature, and *contextual* in approach. They are interested in relating the biblical message to contemporary and existential questions, and lay no claim to a universal perspective. They are concerned with the meaning of the biblical text not in an intellectualist but in an existential sense. The results of their investigations are considered valid for the contexts concerned but with possible validity for other contexts.

Because African readings of the Bible are contextual, and because of the wide diversity of the social, economic, political, and religious contexts of the continent, a large variety of reading methods and strategies have been developed in the last few years. Elsewhere I have identified and analyzed these methods as: comparative studies, evaluative studies, Africa-in-the-Bible studies, feminist/womanist hermeneutics, liberation hermeneutics, black theology, and inculturation hermeneutics.[1] In this paper I intend to discuss the methodology of inculturation hermeneutics, focusing not, as I have done elsewhere, on the interpretation process,[2] but rather on its constitutive elements.

Meaning of Inculturation Hermeneutics

This is a contextual hermeneutic methodology that seeks to make any community of ordinary people and their sociocultural context the *subject* of interpretation of the Bible. Its specific characteristic is that it articulates and emphasizes the use of the conceptual frame of reference of the people doing the reading in the interpretation process. The goal is sociocultural transformation focusing on a variety of situations and issues. Its ethos is cultural diversity and identity in reading practices.

Inculturation hermeneutics has two broad tasks within which there are ramifications. One is appraising the cultural-human dimension of the Bible in respect of its attitude to, and evaluation of, "other" peoples and cultures. The point of departure here is that the Bible is not (culturally and ideologically) an innocent text.[3] It is God's Word in human language, which implies human culture with its ideology, worldview, orientation, perspective, values, and disvalues that are intertwined with the Word of God. This raises the need for a critical ethical reading in terms of its stance toward other peoples and cultures in the light of basic human and biblical values of love and respect for others, justice, peace, unity, and so on. The other task is reading the Bible to appropriate its message for a contemporary context. This involves

1. J. S. Ukpong, "Models and Methods of Biblical Interpretation in Africa," *Neue Zeitschrift für Missionswissenschaft* 55:4 (1999) 279-95.

2. Idem, "Rereading the Bible with African Eyes: Inculturation Hermeneutics," *Journal of Theology for Southern Africa* 83 (1995) 3-14.

3. D. Tracy, *Plurality and Ambiguity: Hermeneutics, Religion, Hope* (San Francisco: Harper & Row, 1987), 79.

engaging a biblical text in dialogue with a contemporary contextual experience so as to appropriate its message in today's context.

I shall here discuss the issues that make up the basic characteristics of this methodology with particular reference to appropriating the biblical message. These issues are: ordinary people as the subject of interpretation, reading with ordinary readers, use of an African conceptual frame of reference in interpretation, the contextual nature of reading, seeing the meaning of a text as a function of the interaction between the text in its context and the present context, a holistic approach to culture, making the biblical message come alive as good news in people's lives, and awareness of functional conditioning of the reader in the process of reading.

Ordinary People and Their Contexts
as the Subject of Interpretation

People (African people in our case), identified socioculturally as groups and defined in terms of their common identities and their concrete, sociohistorical life situations, constitute the *subject* of interpretation of the Bible in the methodology of inculturation hermeneutics. This means more than that these people do the reading. It means that their sociocultural-historical contexts provide the resources for the reading. Basically this involves three elements. One is the use of the people's sociocultural resources as hermeneutical tools of the reading. In our case, these resources include African socioreligious and cultural institutions, thought systems, and practices; African oral narrative genre; African arts and symbols; and so on. Another element is the use of the sociocultural context and worldview of the people as the perspective and background against which the reading is done. This means that the reading is done from the perspective of the people's context and reflects their concerns, values, and interpretive interests. The third element is the use of the people's conceptual frame of reference in the reading. In other words, the conceptual apparatus that informs the reading process is that of the people's culture. This is a crucial element in that it ensures the integrity of both the cultural and ideological identity of the people doing the reading. Without it, the people's cultural identity in the reading becomes highly limited. It is when these three elements function together that the people become fully the subject of the interpretation. Inculturation hermeneutics is characterized by the conjunction of these three elements in its approach.

As a general category the expression "ordinary people" refers to a social class, the common people in contradistinction to the elite. In most of Africa they live by the worldview provided by their traditional cultures: they are poor and marginalized; they suffer economic, social, and political disadvantage; and they are found in both rural and urban areas. They are not trained in the theological sciences; indeed, they are generally illiterate, semiliterate, or functionally illiterate. They have a high sense of self-worth, however, and would not be compromised because of their low social status. Scars of struggle for survival mark their lives. Even though in most cases they live below the subsistence level, they never give up on living (one rarely finds cases of suicide among them). They are "incurably" religious. All these, in different ways, constitute their conditioning in reading. Preference for their insights and life experience as a conditioning in reading does not mean exclusion of the elite; rather it means inviting the elite to be converted to the perspective of the poor and to learn from their experience in reading the Bible.

In contemporary Third World theological discourse, the Bible has often been referred to as a "site of struggle," and the question often arises as to "whose Bible" (whose understanding of the Bible) is to be privileged. In a particular sense the Bible is the site of struggle for control and legitimization between the ordinary people, the church, and the academy. In inculturation hermeneutics the primacy of the reading activity is located not among individual theologians working in isolation but among theologians working within communities of ordinary people — it is the ordinary people that are accorded the epistemological privilege. The Bible is seen as a collection of the ordinary people's experience of God in their lives and communities reflected upon and expressed in stories, prayers, and so on. For this reason, the experience of ordinary people today that share existential conditions and experiences similar to those reflected in the Bible is seen to demand a privileged position in understanding the Bible. This is not to deny the hand of the elite in organizing and presenting the biblical material, and introducing their ideological positions into the text in the process. Rather, it is the awareness of this that has influenced the denial of the epistemological privilege to the elite to avoid a reinforcement of elite ideology in the reading. Bypassing such ideology is seen to be possible when the epistemological privilege is given to ordinary people. In that way the interests of ordinary people come to dominate the agenda for a liberating reading.

Reading with Ordinary Readers

A major way of giving the epistemological privilege to the poor in a manner that produces critical readings is for trained readers to "read with" ordinary people. Thus in inculturation hermeneutics the ivory tower mentality that sees the academy as remote from ordinary people is eschewed, and the readings of ordinary people are seen as significant in the production of the meaning of a text. Rather than make interpretation of the Bible the preserve of scholars, this method accepts the validity of the contribution of ordinary people in the process of biblical interpretation.

Reading "with" means that the reading agenda is that of the community and not of trained readers, that trained readers do not direct or control the reading process or seek to "teach" to the community the meaning of the text that they have already known. Rather, they read as part of the community, and facilitate the interactive process that leads to the community producing a critical meaning of the text. It is a collaborative reading process that transforms and enlarges the subjectivity of readers through hearing and appropriating the text with people whose personal experiences and insights are different from one's own. It implies the recognition and affirmation of the otherness and per-

21

sonal worth of the others.[4] Through such a process academic readers access the resources of popular readings of the Bible, and academic scholarship is informed and enriched by resources outside its own circle, while ordinary readers acquire the perspective of critical reading.

Reading "with" ordinary readers also entails reading "from" their perspective, which implies several things. First, the community reflects on its context in interaction with the text set in its sociohistorical context using the appropriate conceptual frame of reference. Second, the trained readers know and share the cultural perspectives of the community; they situate themselves within the community. It would be impossible for them to use the resources of the people's culture for reading if they did not possess adequate knowledge of and competence in it. Elsewhere I have referred to this as meaning that the trained readers should be "insiders" in the culture,[5] that is, people with adequate knowledge of and competence in the culture. They do not have to be indigenous to the culture. Knowledge of other cultural perspectives and methods of reading by the trained readers is indispensable, because these function as a point of reference for self-criticism. Third, as a matter of priority, questions are put to the text from the perspectives of the most disadvantaged characters (generally whose voices are not "heard" or are passive) in the text. Questions are also posed from the perspectives of the other characters to complement these. A fourth implication that flows from the above is the concern to bring out the "voices" of the unimportant characters that may sometimes be present only thematically in the text.

Reading "with" ordinary readers has meant creating critical reading masses and building communities of faith that read the Bible critically. It is a mode of reading that makes it possible to overcome the predominance of the elite ideology in biblical interpretation.

4. See D. Patte, *Ethics of Biblical Interpretation* (Louisville: Westminster, 1995), 25, 33 n. 21; G. C. Spivak, "Can the Subaltern Speak?" in C. Nelson and L. Grossberg, eds., *Marxism and the Interpretation of Culture* (Urbana: University of Illinois Press, 1988), 295.

5. Ukpong, "Rereading," 5.

Use of an African Conceptual
Frame of Reference in Reading

A distinguishing feature of inculturation hermeneutics is its emphasis on using an African conceptual frame of reference in interpreting the Bible in Africa rather than using another conceptual frame for interpretation and applying the result in the African context. Every reading activity entails three elements that function together: the reading practice itself, the reading method that is used, and the conceptual frame of reference on which both the reading method and practice are grounded.

Reading practices involve putting into operation some reading methods. No one reads the Bible without using some method, whether scientific or unscientific, albeit unconsciously, even if they are untrained Bible readers.[6] However, the reading operation itself is not just the application of a reading method to read a text; it involves the *implementation* of the regime of the method in a particular way directed by particular interests and concerns of both the method and the readers.[7] Readers, most often unconsciously, go to texts with some questions in mind reflecting the interests they have unconsciously imbibed over the years as well as some expectations derived from their preunderstandings, and are influenced by their status in society, denominational affiliation, gender, and so on, in the way they understand texts. Thus different readers may use the same method of reading but arrive at different results. It is at this level that we locate the differences we find, for example, in feminist readings as opposed to androcentric male readings, readings by the poor as opposed to readings by the materially comfortable, readings by those in power as opposed to readings by those under power, readings by the elite as opposed to readings by the lower class, even though all these may be using the same methods.

A *reading method* embodies a procedure along with a conceptual

---

6. Untrained Bible readers unconsciously follow the methods of other Bible readers they have heard or read with the ideology, concerns, and biases that accompany those methods.

7. Patte, *Ethics*, 59.

apparatus with its particular set of cultural (political, social, economic, etc.) and interpretive interests. It comprises theoretical assumptions about the meaning of texts, the nature and purpose of reading, and the world of the reader. It is a child of a particular culture and is founded on a particular conceptual frame of reference. (Every method therefore needs to be criticized to discover its basic assumptions and interpretive interests.) For example, the historical-critical method is a child of the culture of the Enlightenment and the Industrial Revolution. It is informed by the interest to search for historical truth devoid of the intervention of human or divine authority; this kind of search is one of the ideals of the Enlightenment. In its positivistic form, it involves bracketing out the presence of the supernatural in the Bible. Inculturation hermeneutics is informed by the ideals of African culture. It seeks to make the message of the Bible come alive in contemporary contexts, and is strongly affirmative of the presence of the supernatural in the Bible.

A *conceptual frame of reference* is a mental apparatus. It refers to the type of understanding of the universe that informs the reading, that is, the mind-set that is at work in the reading operation. It comprises a particular set of worldviews, values, disvalues, and basic assumptions about reality. It forms the basic foundation of any reading method, informs the method and the reading practice in which the method is used, and is acquired imperceptibly through the use of the method. It is, at bottom, the grid through which the biblical text is read. (It is important then to criticize every reading method to discover the conceptual frame of reference that informs it.) Classical Western reading methods and practices are informed by the Western conceptual frame of reference, while inculturation hermeneutics is informed by the African conceptual frame of reference. The difference between the two is significant. For example, within the African conceptual frame of reference, the reality of the interaction between the supernatural and natural worlds, the spirit world and the world of physical human existence, and the interconnectedness of all these, are taken for granted, while that is not the case in the Western conceptual frame of reference. Other characteristics of the Western conceptual frame of reference include dualism, individualism, historicism, and intellectualism, while a unitive view of reality, emphasis on community, and pragmatic outlook are among the marks of the African conceptual frame of reference.[8]

In any reading practice, the conceptual frame of reference used may be that of the reader's cultural community or of another.[9] When, for example, Africans *uncritically* use the historical-critical method, which is informed by the Western conceptual frame of reference, they are using another cultural community's conceptual grid to read.[10] An important aspect of inculturation hermeneutics is the use, in the interpretation process, of the conceptual frame of reference of the community within which interpretation is done. Thus in inculturation hermeneutics, texts are not appropriated with a foreign conceptual frame of reference and then applied to the African context; rather, an African conceptual frame of reference is used in appropriating the text. Historical tools are used critically and made to function within the African conceptual frame of reference. In that way the African people and their contexts are made the *subject* of the interpretation.

8. See P. A. Talbot, *Life in Southern Nigeria* (London: Macmillan, 1923), 140; P. Tempels, *African Philosophy* (Paris: Présence Africaine, 1956), 25; G. Lienhardt, *Divinity and Experience: The Religion of the Dinka* (Oxford: Oxford University Press, 1961), 28; J. S. Mbiti, *African Religions and Philosophy* (London: University of London Press, 1970), 97; K. C. Anyanwu, "The African World-View and Theory of Knowledge," in E. A. Ruch and K. C. Anyanwu, eds., *African Philosophy: An Introduction to the Main Philosophical Trends in Contemporary Africa* (Rome: Catholic Book Agency, 1981), 90-93; E. Ikenga-Metuh, *God and Man in African Religion* (London: Geoffrey Chapman, 1981), 52.

9. R. Bailey, "The Danger of Ignoring One's Own Cultural Bias in Interpreting the Text," in R. S. Sugirtharajah, ed., *The Postcolonial Bible* (Sheffield: Sheffield Academic Press, 1998), 67-90, here 78; S. Fish, *Is There a Text in This Class? The Authority of Interpretive Communities* (Cambridge: Harvard University Press, 1980); W. Iser, *The Act of Reading: A Theory of Aesthetic Response* (Baltimore: Johns Hopkins University Press, 1978); J. P. Tompkins, *Reader-Response Criticism: From Formalism to Post-Structuralism* (Baltimore: Johns Hopkins University Press, 1980).

10. For the difference between critical and uncritical use of the historical method by Africans see J. S. Ukpong, "Can African Old Testament Scholarship Escape the Historical Critical Approach?" *Newsletter on African Old Testament Scholarship* (now *Bulletin for Old Testament Studies in Africa*) 7 (1999) 5.

Contextual Character of Reading

Inculturation hermeneutics is contextual in character, and this refers to the following:

1. The readings are done *from a certain standpoint or perspective.* African readings of the Bible are explicitly perspectival; they do not claim to issue from a universal standpoint. This stems from the fact that in physical terms we, as human beings, can stand at only one location at a time when viewing things. Similarly, in epistemological terms, the human mind is not granted the possibility of multi- or universal location in the process of intellection. It is always limited to a certain location that provides the "angle of vision" for understanding. Biblical interpretation practices in Africa are based on this simple experience and therefore do not claim to be universal. Thus they explicitly state the context of their interpretation, that is, the location from which the interpretation takes place.

2. The readings do not claim to appropriate the totality of the meaning of the texts read. This is based on the theory that in any given reading only *a certain aspect or certain aspects of a text* get appropriated. By virtue of the limitation of our human nature, it is not possible to appropriate all aspects of a text at once; only a certain aspect is accessible to us in any reading process, depending on our standpoint. In other words, a text has more aspects, dimensions, and perspectives than we see and appropriate in any given reading.[11] As a corollary, the more perspectival readings of a text we are aware of, the more dimensions of the text are disclosed to us, and the better we can appreciate it.

3. The readings are done in *relation to some context outside the Bible itself.* Human knowledge does not take place in a vacuum but always in relation to other things in the external world. New things are known through a process of relating them to things we already

11. Patte, *Ethics,* 37-65.

know. Making meaning of a biblical text involves relating the text to some empirical experience we have in the world outside the Bible. Thus the meaning we have is contextual, that is, it is produced through relating the text with something else that we already know. This may happen implicitly or explicitly.

4. The readings are mediated through a particular *conceptual frame of reference* derived from the worldview and the sociocultural context of a particular cultural community. This differs from community to community. It informs and shapes the exegetical methodology and the reading practice and acts as a grid for making meaning of the text.

On the basis of these considerations, every reading is regarded as contextual; and readings that claim to be universal remain suspect and are seen as attempts to universalize the particular. African readings therefore do not claim to be universal; they are explicitly contextual and particular. However, such particular readings are not exclusivist or closed, but are open to "conversation" with other forms of reading.

Location of Meaning in Texts

In inculturation hermeneutics, the meaning of a text is seen as a function of the interaction between the text studied in its sociohistorical context on the one hand, and the sociocultural context of the readers on the other. The purpose of interpretation is to appropriate a text's meaning in a contemporary sociocultural context. Biblical texts are seen as rooted in their historical contexts yet as plurivalent, capable of speaking to different situations and contexts across time and space.[12] Thus the hermeneutical process involves four poles that interplay: the text, the context of the text, the reading community, and the context of the reading community. Meaning is understood as *produced* in the pro-

12. J. S. Croatto, *Biblical Hermeneutics: Toward a Theory of Reading as the Production of Meaning* (Maryknoll, N.Y.: Orbis, 1987), 19.

cess of a *community* of ordinary readers within their *sociocultural context* reading *the text* against its *sociohistorical context*. Both the contemporary sociocultural context and the sociohistorical context of the text are analyzed to establish a meaningful relationship between them. Because the historical context of any text has many ramifications, directions, and dimensions to it, the contemporary context is analyzed first to identify the specific issue(s) to be reflected upon in the reading. Thus methodological priority is given to the context of the readers.[13] This enables the readers to establish a focus for historical research, and to clarify for themselves the sort of questions to put to the text. The validity of readings is judged by their faithfulness to the ethical demands of the gospel that include love of neighbor, respect for one another, and so on.

Inculturation hermeneutics therefore involves interpreting a text in terms of the present but not in isolation from the past. It recognizes that though given in specific historical contexts in the past, the biblical message transcends the particularity of its context and becomes part of our world today and can therefore speak to the present. Simply put, then, within the context of inculturation hermeneutics, interpreting a text means putting it in interaction between its sociohistorical context and our own context and making it address and question our context.[14]

Holistic Approach to Culture

The idea of culture is a conceptual construct generally agreed to be a tool for clarifying identity and difference in the human community. Its definition is today highly contested. It is understood here not just as signifying practices[15] but also as the totality of the way of life of a human com-

13. I. J. Mosala, *Biblical Hermeneutics and Black Theology in South Africa* (Grand Rapids: Eerdmans, 1989), 123-25.

14. V. L. Wimbush, "Biblical-Historical Study as Liberation: Toward An Afro-Christian Hermeneutic," *Journal of Religious Thought* 42:2 (1985-86) 19.

15. J. Storey, *Cultural Theory and Popular Culture*, 2d ed. (Athens, Ga.: University of Georgia Press, 1998), 2.

munity. Thus the activities of any given human community, whether they be social, political, economic, religious, leisure activities, the arts, textual productions, reading practices, and so on, all belong in the realm of cultural practices. Besides, culture is seen as having two dimensions — secular/material and sacred/religious — that affect one another in an interlacing manner that makes any discourse within one dimension impinge on the other. Within this conspectus, therefore, no issue may be seen as purely secular or purely religious. Every issue has both a secular and a religious dimension to it. Culture is also the medium for interpreting the world, for self-expression and self-understanding. It emerges through human interaction within a community (it is not a matter of external and ingenious human contrivance), and is dynamic and open-ended. The holistic understating of culture recognizes the importance and the contribution of the ordinary and commonplace in the production of knowledge. It bypasses the ideological separation of the popular from the elite, the traditional from the modern, in cultures, accepting all as legitimate objects of inquiry.[16] This understanding of culture makes it possible to raise, within the ambit of inculturation hermeneutics, a variety of issues — justice issues of gender, race, social, economic, and political oppression as well as issues of indigenous cultural and religious identity, customs, and practices.

Making the Biblical Message Come Alive as Good News in People's Lives

African life and thought emphasizes the concrete aspects of life rather than the theoretical, and the pragmatic rather than the speculative. (This does not of course mean denying the theoretical or speculative in African thought.) This has influenced the approach in the methodology of inculturation hermeneutics such that the biblical message is not looked upon as moral propositions to be assented to in theory, but as

---

16. C. Mukerji and M. Schudson, *Rethinking Popular Culture: Contemporary Perspectives in Cultural Studies* (Berkeley: University of California Press, 1991), 2.

good news to be actualized in the daily lives of people. Hence Bible readings are concerned to make the biblical message come alive as good news in people's lives, in church life, and in the society at large, and thus transform the readers and their society. Besides, they are inserted within the dynamics of the people's committed action and seek to articulate the people's experience of their life in Christ as well as provide insights for reflecting on such experience. They are concerned about integration of reflection and practice, and are life-centered. They seek to appropriate the biblical message not in abstract theoretical terms but within the context of a commitment to action in concrete human situations. The goal is not merely to acquire knowledge about the Bible but to facilitate the living of the Christian faith in concrete life situations and to provide answers to questions of practical life concerns from the perspectives of the questioners. The focus, for example, is not on God in an abstract way or on God who relates to people in a vague general way, but on God who relates to people in their specific sociocultural and historical contexts. Readers are not mere armchair theoreticians but active pastoral agents who are involved in the life of the community. In this way the Word of God is not presented as mere theory but is made to find expression in the concrete aspects of the people's life of commitment to action. Thus, ideally, from this perspective, academic Bible reading is seen to be inadequate if it is not inserted within the dynamics of a people's committed action.

Inculturation hermeneutic readings issue from a deep commitment to the Christian faith. The Bible is seen as a classic and a sacred text, and both aspects are seen as complementary. As classical literature, it is a cultural product that can be investigated like any other literature, and read using the techniques of secular literary practices. It is thus amenable to critical scrutiny and scholarly debate. However, such investigation is seen not as a means of destroying the sacred character of the Bible, but of enhancing interaction of its sacred dimension with contemporary secular reality. As a sacred text, the Bible is seen as having a moral authority and is taken as a spiritual and moral guide to life. It is God's liberating Word that is still alive, having great significance for humanity and therefore needing to be actualized in the community.

Interpreting the Bible thus means unleashing the liberating message of God to be experienced as good news in the concrete in human society. Thus the message of the Bible is appropriated with the resources of the culture to nourish as well as challenge life within the society.

Transcending the Functional Conditioning of Readers

In inculturation hermeneutics the role of the personal conditioning of the readers in reading practices is recognized, and it is required that it be articulated and used critically. "Personal conditioning" has to do with how the subjectivity of the reader is constructed, and involves factors that are economic, religious, social, political, ideological, gendered, racial — worldview. Every form of conditioning has both positive and negative effects depending on whether they constitute liberative or oppressive practices. For example, with regard to gender differentiation, male-dominated readings of certain texts of the Bible have often produced results that oppress women, or that are not sympathetic to women's cause, while feminist hermeneutics has led to new and liberative readings of such texts. Also, biases and predetermined positions such as racial prejudice, the religious confession of the readers, and so on, may produce oppressive readings, but they could also be used to subvert such readings. The conditioning works like lenses through which readings are filtered; it gives colors to the reading. No reader or reading community is free from it; but the situation is transcended by recognizing these conditions and using them creatively, and by reflecting in a community. Inculturation hermeneutics emphasizes the need to be critically aware of these personal conditions, and to articulate and use them critically and positively in the interpretation process.

Conclusion

The inculturation movement arose in Africa out of the attempt to bring the resources of African culture into the appropriation of the

Christian message and make the Word of God come alive in African society. Over the years various approaches of this movement have appeared. The above represent the basic elements of a holistic approach of inculturation methodology. The distinctive characteristic of this approach is its emphasis on making the African context the *subject* of interpretation of the Christian message through the use of the people's conceptual frame of reference in the interpretation process. It also embodies a holistic understanding of culture whereby both secular and religious issues in society are seen as interrelated, and critical ideological questions are raised in the process of reading the Bible. It is a methodology that facilitates "reading with" ordinary readers.

In the context of doing theology and reading the Bible in Africa, Desmond Tutu has remarked that Africans had for long been fed with answers to questions they never asked.[17] In so far as biblical interpretation involves putting questions to the biblical text and getting answers from it, the methodology of inculturation hermeneutics seeks to ensure that the questions and concerns of African readers (and for that matter any cultural group of readers) come to the fore in the academic investigation of the Bible, and that the answers are given from the perspectives from which these questions arise.

17. D. Tutu, "Whither African Theology?" in E. W. Fashole-Luke, et al., eds., *Christianity in Independent Africa* (Bloomington: Indiana University Press, 1978), 336.

EGO AND SELF IN THE
NEW TESTAMENT AND IN ZEN

Seiichi Yagi

The Japanese Context

To begin with, I would like to recall the Japanese philosophical background in which the dialogue between Buddhists and Christians came
into being. The philosopher Kitaro Nishida (1870-1945) was the first to
express the Zen view of reality in a philosophical way.[1] First, he wanted
to describe what is revealed to the awakened eye. However, he faced the
problem of "what I am," that is, what the subject of this description is.
In order to see it one has to awake to that. The subject that awoke to itself would then become fully aware of the "transcendence." He expressed this by saying: "The individuals are set in the absolute so that
the individual and the absolute form a unity." This "being one" he
called *basho* in Japanese or *topos* in Greek, that is, "field," or better,
"sphere." In that sense humanity is in the "Topos." With this thesis he
became the founder of the so-called Kyoto school of Zen philosophy.

1. Among his most important works translated into English are: K. Nishida,
Fundamental Problems of Philosophy, Monumenta Nipponica 36 (Tokyo: Sophia University Press, 1970); idem, *Intelligibility and the Philosophy of Nothingness* (Westport,
Conn.: Greenwood, 1973); idem, *A Study of Good* (repr. New York: Greenwood, 1988);
idem, *Intuition and Reflection in Self-Consciousness* (Albany: State University of New
York Press, 1987); idem, *Last Writings: Nothingness and the Religious Worldview* (Hono-
lulu: University of Hawaii Press, 1987). In German are available: K. Nishida, *Die intelli-
gible Welt* (Berlin: de Gruyter, 1943); idem, *Logik des Ortes: Der Anfang der modernen
Philosophie in Japan* (Darmstadt: Wissenschaftliche Buchgesellschaft, 1999).

His student Keiji Nishitani (1900-1990) occupied himself a lot with German mysticism.[2] He also expounded on the Topos philosophy of his teacher Nishida. "Topos," according to him, became the sphere of the transcendent-immanent power. The individuals in the "sphere" are such that they permeate each other infinitely. This sphere is a genuine Buddhist expression for śunyatā, that is, the void. Individuals are, therefore, not like the atom in the classic sense of the word. For they have their identity in their mutual relations.

A great deal links individuals and the sphere as such: states, cultures, positive religions, and so on. Shizuteru Ueda, a third-generation philosopher of the Kyoto school,[3] wants to do justice to this point. For him, humans exist in the world, as Martin Heidegger put it. A human's being is "worry."[4] This, however, is only one side of things. The other side, according to Ueda, is that this "human, and the world in which humanity is, are both in the 'Topos,'" that is, in the "sphere" where everything is open toward transcendence and mutual relations. Therefore, a human's "being" in the "Topos" is not defined only by "worry," as was the case according to Heidegger, but also by freedom from "worry." Thus Ueda combines Nishida and Heidegger and calls this the teaching of the "dual world." Ueda's model of thinking is represented in the table of "Correspondences" (on p. 35) in the third row from the bottom (line 6).

This, however, is a formulation also accessible to Christian thinkers. If one interprets it in a Christian way, "God" corresponds to what Ueda calls "Topos." We can interpret Ueda in a Christian way: Humans

---

2. In English are available: K. Nishitani, *Religion and Nothingness,* Nanzen Studies in Religion and Culture 2 (Berkeley: University of California Press, 1982); idem, *The Self-overcoming of Nihilism* (Albany: State University of New York Press, 1990); in German is available: idem, *Was ist Religion?* (Frankfurt: Insel, 1982).

3. None of his books has been translated into English. In German are available: S. Ueda, *Die Gottesgeburt in der Seele und der Durchbruch zur Gottheit,* Studien zur Religion, Geschichte und Geisteswissenschaft 31 (Gütersloh: Mohn, 1965); idem, *Luther und Shinran — Eckart und Zen* (Leiden: Brill, 1989). Cf. furthermore: idem, "Das Erwachen im Zen-Buddhismus als Wort-Ereignis," in W. Strolz and S. Ueda, eds., *Offenbarung als Heilserfahrung in Christentum, Hinduismus und Buddhismus,* Schriften zur Grossen Oekumene 8 (Freiburg: Stiftung Oratio Dominica, 1982), 209-34.

4. M. Heidegger, *Being and Time,* part I, chap. 6.

CORRESPONDENCES

G= God; M= Man; W= World; MW= Man and World together

	G / [G in MW] as primordial fact	[G in MW] activated in M	M in W	[M in W] in G: [G in MW] is not activated in M	[M in W] in G: [G in MW] is activated in M
1. Anthropology		Self	Ego	Mere Ego, to whom the Self is not showing itself	Self-Ego, to whom and in whom the Self is showing itself
2. Christology	G Logos	Christ in me	Jesus		Jesus Christ
3. Takizawa	G The primordial contact of God with man	Awakening to God [G in MW]		"Ego" in the primordial contact with man	The secondary contact of God with man
4. Jesus	G Reign of God, Son of Man		Ego	(e.g., Pharisee of Luke 18:10ff)	"Ego" as representative of the Son of Man
5. Paul	G Son of God	Christ	Ego	Ego of Rom 7:7-24	Self (Christ in me) — Ego (Gal 2:20)
6. Ueda	Topos	Topos	M in W (Ego)	Ego	[M in W] in Topos = Ego in the Dual World
7. Suzuki; Akizuki	Transindividuum	Transindividuum	Individuum	Individuum	Individuum qua Transindividuum
8. Trikāya-Doctrine	Dharma-kāya	Sambhoga-kāya	Gautama		Nirmāṇa-kāya Gautama Buddha

are in the world, and both are in God. (God in Christianity is the ultimate agent as well as the ultimate "Topos.") We therefore have three or four basic words: humanity, world, and "Topos" or "God." And we have two basic categories: the "being-in-the-world" and the "being-in-God" or "being-in-the-Topos." By combining these basic words and basic categories we still cannot define many important concepts of the philosophy of religion or of theology, but at least we can locate them.

I would now like to draw attention to the Christian thinker Katsumi Takizawa (1909-1984).[5] He became the pioneer concerning the dialogue between Christianity and Buddhism in Japan. Takizawa was a student of Kitaro Nishida and Karl Barth. His basic thesis was: No matter what one is or is not, and unaffected by whether one has a religion, and which religion, one has an underlying foundation as the basis of being oneself. This is the primordial fact of "Immanuel," that is, "God with us." This primordial fact states that humanity is in God. Takizawa also called this primordial fact "unity of God and humanity" or "Christ." Not every human being is aware of this primordial fact. Only when one is awakened to it does a conscious religious life come about. Takizawa called this primordial fact "God's primary contact with humanity," and the religious life evolved by awakening to it he called "God's secondary contact with humanity" (see table on p. 35). What is it in humanity that is awakened to it? Technically one could say: It is the human "I" that is awakened. What this means we will see in more detail later.

By differentiating between God's primary and secondary contact with humanity, Takizawa criticized the traditional Christology: for him, Jesus is a human being who has realized in an exemplary manner God's secondary contact with humanity. But he himself is not the primary contact. The primary contact did not come into existence in and through Jesus. Rather, the primary contact is the eternal and universal primordial fact "Immanuel." Jesus is a human being like Gautama Bud-

---

5. None of his books has been translated into English. In German are available: K. Takizawa, *Reflexionen über die universale Grundlage von Buddhismus und Christentum*, Studien zur interkulturellen Geschichte des Christentums 24 (Frankfurt: M. Lang, 1980); idem, *Das Heil im Jetzt*, Theologie der Ökumene 21 (Göttingen: Vandenhoeck & Ruprecht, 1987).

dha, who in the Indian tradition has realized in an exemplary manner God's secondary contact. Buddhism and Christianity are two typical expressions of God's secondary contact with humanity. They are, so to speak, sister religions. I am one of those — among Christians relatively few — who agree with Takizawa.

We can, after Takizawa, develop his christological differentiation in two directions:

1. When a human is awakened to the primordial fact, it is activated and realized in him or her. That means that the awakening and the realization take place simultaneously. Before awakening, the primordial fact remains potential. Faith in Christ gives the believer an awakened understanding of oneself. In this sense Christianity, too, knows awakening or enlightenment (2 Cor 4:6). The Christian becomes aware of the fact that Christ lives in one (Gal 2:20; cf. Rom 8:10). "Faith" and "awakening" or enlightenment are parallel, basic expressions that describe the relationship between God and humanity.

2. The activated, primordial fact is divine-human ("Christ in me"), as we will see even more clearly later. What then is "God" in so far as he is one with the world and humanity? God is in this respect the universal Logos. And in contrast to the Logos, "Christ" is the activated and realized Logos in humanity. In that sense "Christ" is the "incarnated Logos." In Christology we have to differentiate between the human being Jesus and the primordial fact "Immanuel" or "Christ." Likewise, we have to differentiate between the universal Logos, the universal reality, and "Christ" as the divine-human in humanity. Differentiating like that, one can also compare the universal Logos to the last reality in Buddhism, the Dharma, the foundation of Buddhaness. By that, the parallelism between both religions becomes more evident.

For those who know Buddhism, I want to add the following: If we do differentiate between Logos, Christ, and Jesus, this also corresponds to the so-called Trikāya teaching, the Buddhist doctrine of Buddha's three ways of being.[6] The first is "Dharma-kāya," the universal foundation of Buddha being; this corresponds in Christian terms to the universal Logos. The second is "Saṃbhoga-kāya," the personal Buddha who works in the world and in humankind for salvation, that is, awakening. He corresponds to Christ. The third is "Nirmāṇa-kāya," the incarnated Dharma-kāya, for example, Gautama Buddha, who corresponds to the human being Jesus.

In the following section, I continue to explain the "primordial fact" "Immanuel" = "God with us," as Takizawa calls it: the common nucleus of the Christian and the Buddhist religions. I would like to show that this "God with us" is not to be understood in the sense of a substantial unity between God and humanity, but as oneness of divine and human activities, which enables at the same time an immediate experience of the divine-human unity of human existence. In my third section, I would like to show how we can express this nucleus more precisely with anthropological concepts by distinguishing between "Self" and "Ego."

"God-with-Us" as "Oneness of Divine and Human Activities"

The common nucleus of Christianity and Buddhism is what Buddhists call the "realized Buddha nature," and what Christians call "Christ who lives in me" (Gal 2:20). In order to notice this, "awakening" (as Buddhists call it) has to occur in the human subject. It is not merely an everyday experience, because by it a subject exchange takes place: the exchange from the "mere ego" to the "Self-ego." I am going to explain these terms later on. For the present, it is important only that the new "Self-ego" is located not within the human mind or intellect but in the body.

The human being is body. I do not "have" a body, I *am* body. The body is not only a vessel for reason or an instrument of the ego. Reason

6. Cf. the table of "Correspondences," p. 35, line 8.

is rather an organ, a function, of the body. The person is neither the body in which the divine-eternal soul is locked up nor the individual whose being is reason, but the person is the whole body, which understands itself and communicates with others. By that I have outlined the basic convictions of the biblical and Buddhist understanding of humanity.

In that respect, Friedrich Nietzsche has to be given preference over the rationalism that represents a mainstream of Western thinking. Unfortunately, however, Nietzsche saw the nature of life in the will to power. But the body is meant to live with others because the body is the site of relations. The body is part of the world and of life; it is interwoven in the history of the living things. As person, the body is the local sphere in which interaction takes place, a pole that cannot exist without its opposite pole, a pole therefore whose identity consists in its relation with others. Because the person is the body, which understands itself and communicates with others, it is destined to live together; and to live together means concretely to address and respond to others in family life but also in economic-political, sociocultural life, and, finally, in religious life. These ways of life are necessary because we are one body.

We want to interpret Ueda's teaching of the dual world in a Christian way: a human is in the world as body, which in turn is in God. Here we find implicated not only the unity of God and world (nature, living beings), but also the unity of God and humanity. If a human is in God as a body that is in unity with God, and if the body as material and life is one with God, how can the material world and the living beings not be one with God? Jesus says no sparrow falls to the ground apart from God (Matt 10:29), and the reign of God is like the soil that produces fruit by itself (Mark 4:26-29). This oneness, however, is not substantial, but functional. It is the oneness of divine and human activities.

"Love comes from God. Everyone who loves has been born of God and knows God" (1 John 4:7).[7] Human love is born by God's

---

7. Unless otherwise noted, all Bible citations are from *The Holy Bible, New International Version* (New York: International Bible Society, 1978).

work. That does not mean that humanity is God, nor that love is God, nor that with love God and humanity work together, but that human love as such originates in God and that humanity's work means a godly deed. Whoever is awakened to this "oneness of divine and human activities" recognizes God's works because of the love one has so that one knows God although one does not see God as an object. Thereby, one becomes fully aware of the "oneness of divine and human activities." We already see that this duality corresponds to the dual world of Ueda's teachings: love is in the world; both are in God.

The "oneness of divine and human activities" is a key concept of Keiji Nishitani's interpretation of Meister Eckhart, who himself talked about it.[8] This concept is, as far as I can see, of crucial importance. The Christian church did avoid talking about the unity of God with humanity. It had to oppose Gnosticism, which stood for the unity of God with humanity. But the Gnostics insisted on the substantial unity, even on the identity, of humanity with God, but not on the "oneness of divine and human activities." It is a misunderstanding of mysticism to think that it stands for the substantial identity of God with humanity and thereby negates human subjectivity. The rejection of the "oneness of divine and human activities," however, causes the loss of the real experience of God's work in humanity, which is the basis of the knowledge of God in Christian faith. We do not experience God directly. We experience oneness of divine-human activities. More correctly, we experience love as such oneness.

Whoever experiences love as divine-human "oneness of divine and human activities" knows God, who works within humanity. God does not reveal himself objectively, but is revealed in whoever has profound self-understanding. By that, God reveals himself to the understanding faith. In the light of this understanding of faith the believing eyes see nature (Luke 12:22-31), history, the individual, and their utterances also as God's address to humanity. In that sense, God is not an object, not even mere immanence, but also a counterpart.

8. K. Nishitani, *God and Absolute Nothingness* (Japanese) (Tokyo: Kobundo, 1948), chap. 2.

From the point of view of the Trinity, God's unity with the world, including humanity, has to do with the second person of the Trinity: God, insofar that he is one with the world (John 1:2) and thus is also one with humanity, is the Logos. On the other hand the world is called creation, or creature, in that it forms a unity with the Logos. Consequently, the second person of the Trinity is not Jesus but the Logos, and the world is understood as that which forms a "oneness of divine and human activities" with the Logos. God's unity with humanity means, in addition, that God is in the world and therefore is working in humanity. As Paul puts it: "for it is God who works in you to will and to act according to his good purpose" (Phil 2:13). A human as body is actually a unity with God in works. And, as was pointed out, this unity has no effect in a person if one is not awakened to it.

The "Individuum qua Transindividuum" or the "Self-Ego"

In the following, I would like to introduce another fundamental idea of Buddhism, the "individuum as transindividuum." This name is given to a human being that has been awakened to the Buddha nature, the human being in whom the Buddha nature is activated. Linzai, a Chinese Zen master from the ninth century, called the person in whom the Buddha nature was activated "the true individual with no status." One can compare this with what Paul calls "the inner humanity" (cf. 2 Cor 4:16).

The great Zen master Daisetsu T. Suzuki and his student Master Ryomin Akizuki called the actualized Buddha nature "the transindividual," and they called the awakened individual as a whole "Individuum qua Transindividuum." Being awakened, then, means to be awakened "to the transindividuum" or to the transindividuality of the body so that a human being understands oneself as "Individuum qua Transindividuum."

The same happens to Paul, to whom and in whom Christ revealed himself (Gal 1:16) and who at the same time believed in Christ (Gal

2:20). He too was "Individuum qua Transindividuum." "Christ in him" (the activated "oneness of divine and human activities") is the transindividual, and the "I" of Paul who believes in him is the individual, so that his person can be understood as "Individuum qua Transindividuum." Because of this, Paul calls the believer "God's temple" (1 Cor 3:16; 6:19).

In order to exemplify the parallelism between the Buddhist transindividual and "Christ in humanity," I cite a Zen dialogue from Tuan times that was often mentioned by D. T. Suzuki and his student R. Akizuki.[9] Once upon a time, when the Zen master Ungan prepared tea, his friend Dogo entered and asked: "Who do you make tea for?" Ungan answered and said: "There is the one who wants to drink tea." Dogo then said: "Can he not make tea for himself?" Ungan said to him: "Fortunately I am here." This story is preceded by a dialogue between Ungan and the famous Zen master Hyakujo, who once said: "If one does not work on a day one should not eat that day." When Ungan visited Hyakujo he was working. Ungan asked Hyakujo and said to him, "Most Honorable, who do you work for so diligently every day?" Hyakujo answered and said: "There is the one who needs my work." Ungan asked, "Why do you not make him work himself?" Hyakujo answered: "He alone cannot accomplish anything."

Master R. Akizuki commented on this and said: The "one" who the masters worked for is the transindividual, whereas the "I" that worked for the transindividual is the individual. Therefore the Zen masters were "Individuum qua Transindividuum." This does not mean, however, that the transindividual would just be a bodily need such as thirst. It rather means that the masters were "Individuum qua Transindividuum" even when they were occupied with the most common bodily labor.

I return to Paul. He says: "I will not venture to speak of anything except what Christ has accomplished through me" (Rom 15:18). Therefore, his mission was what Christ accomplished through him. This is a

9. R. Akizuki, *The Absolute Nothingness and Topos* (Japanese) (Tokyo: Seido Sha, 1996), 381-86.

typical example of the "oneness of divine and human activities."[10] In that sense we can picture an imaginary scene. Somebody comes to Paul and asks him: "What are you doing, Paul?" Paul answers and says to him: "I am preaching Christ." The person asks: "Why do you do that?" Paul answers: "Christ wants to be preached." The person continues: "Paul, let Christ do that for himself!" But Paul answers and says: "Christ alone cannot accomplish that. Fortunately I am here." The Pauline "Christ," therefore, corresponds to the transindividual, and the "I" of Paul is the individual, and Paul can be called "Individuum qua Transindividuum."

To name the awakened people, Ungan used two words: "the One" (the transindividual) and "I" (the individual). In the following I want to state this even more precisely by using a conceptual differentiation of C. G. Jung. However, the differentiation has been made actually often, for example, in Buddhist tradition: the differentiation between "Self" and "ego."[11] We call the "transindividuum" the "Self," and the "individual" the I, the "ego." Considering this, "being awakened" means that the "Self" shows itself to and in the "ego" so that the "ego" becomes fully aware of the "Self" and consciously expresses this "Self." Paul puts it this way: "Christ lives in me" (Gal 2:20). "Christ" means the last subject of "me," that is, the "Self." In contrast to that the "I" that believes in Christ is the "ego." The revelation of the Son (Gal 1:16) means that the Self showed itself to and in the ego so that the ego has become fully aware of this. Paul as ego believes in the Son of God, and faith is born by the works of Christ within him. Consequently, one can call Paul not only "Individuum qua Transindividuum" but also "Self-ego."

The divine-human Self is transindividual: Christ in Paul is at the same time Christ who is in every believer (Rom 8:10). The whole church is the body of Christ (1 Cor 12). In that sense, Christ who is in every believer can at the same time be personified as a transindividual figure and be the object of faith. Especially in Christianity the trans-

---

10. In this case the oneness of activities is seen not between God and humanity, but between the Transindividuum (Self, "Christ in me") and the individuum (ego).

11. Cf. the table of "Correspondences," p. 35, line 1.

individual dimension is important, because in Christianity the church is central. The church needs a transindividual center that it believes in. Zen Buddhism, on the contrary, concerns itself mainly with the clarification of "being oneself." The Zen Buddhist becomes fully aware of the transindividuum in him or her. That is why Zen Buddhism tends toward "atheism": it rejects the merely objective God who is not working within humanity.

With our conceptual differentiation much can be clarified. One example is the expression "Son of Man." The "Son of Man" (i.e., the Son of God as eschatological figure) can be interpreted as Jesus' "Self," whereas Jesus' "I" is the "ego." Jesus can say that what he does is the deed of the Son of Man (Self) in and through him (ego). He understands himself as the representative of the Son of Man: "If anyone is ashamed of me and my words in this adulterous and sinful generation, the Son of Man will be ashamed of him when he comes in his Father's glory with the holy angels" (Mark 8:38). The expression "Son of Man," to me, does not mean that Jesus as a man himself would be the superhuman Son of Man. No, it only expresses the oneness activities of Jesus (ego) and the Son of Man in him (Self) to which Jesus was awakened. Jesus says, too, the "Son of Man" is Lord even of the Sabbath (Mark 2:28), just as if he himself were the Son of Man. He is not, but we also see here his understanding of himself that in and through him (ego) the Son of Man (Self) acts. We do not, for instance, have to assume a mistake in the translation from Aramaic. If in Aramaic the expression "Son of Man" stands at the same time also for "I" and "human being," there could hardly have been a better expression for Jesus' understanding of himself. Considering Jesus, one can say that the "Son of Man" is the "Self" or the "transindividuum." In my understanding of Jesus, the "Son of Man" is the personification of the reign of God in him, the kingdom of God that works in humanity and through humanity so that humanity acts without self-interest or worry. The Good Samaritan (Luke 10:30-37) is the best example.

The "Son of Man" according to Jesus corresponds to the "Christ" according to Paul. The "Son of Man" or "Christ" works in and through Jesus or Paul. Both of them are transindividual or collective, transcendent-immanent. Both are the Son of God who appears at the end of time from heaven. According to both Jesus and Paul, the eschaton is the image of the victory of God's reign. However, there are also differences. Paul never talks as if he were Christ. He mentions Jesus in the third person, whereas Jesus acted as if he himself were the "Son of Man." It is remarkable that great Zen masters act similarly when they know that their behavior comes from the transindividual — of course, through the ego. Once, Shin-ichi Hisamatsu, a great Zen master and Zen thinker, told me in conversation: "I do not die." What he meant by that became clear on another occasion when he told me: "I am old. I can die any minute. When I am dead please continue the conversation with me who is in you." Hisamatsu could speak as a representative of Dharma.

The opposite of the "Self-ego" is the "mere ego." It is the ego that knows nothing of the Self and relies only on itself without consideration of others. The ego is self-conscious because without self-consciousness self-control is impossible. The mere self-conscious ego looks also at itself, to be precise, with a concentrated self-consciousness, which is concerned only with itself. It judges itself by its own criteria set by itself. The mere ego compares itself with others, and if it is pleased with itself it proudly looks down upon them. It does so because being able to be proud and content is its main interest.

The Pharisee in Luke 18:9-14 is such an ego. He takes pride in his flawless, law-abiding accomplishments. It might be true that he kept all laws perfectly. But his words "God, I thank you that I am not like this tax collector," show that he is interested only in himself. Other people exist only to boost his pride. The tax collector may have done a lot of evil, indeed. But his words "God, have mercy on me, a sinner," do not spring from his mere ego, but out of the Self. The mere ego cannot know its own sin. In those days a tax collector could have boasted and said that he, collecting taxes for the Romans, protected his people from the attack of the Romans, so that his people should thank him.

Prior to his conversion, Paul used to be a person just like that Pharisee. He considered only himself. He thought his obedience to the law was important. He compared himself with his contemporaries and was probably proud of himself (Gal 1:14). The Christian Paul, on the other hand, is freed from such self-consciousness. He says: "For I am not conscious of myself" (1 Cor 4:4).[12] This does not mean that he would not have a bad conscience if he examined himself inwardly and outwardly. He says: "He who judges me is the Lord."[13] He no longer takes an interest in himself.

The mere ego that is in principle concerned only with itself and compares itself with others is unavoidably full of such emotions like wickedness, evil, greed, depravity, envy, murder, strife, deceit, malice, and so on, as Paul lists them in Rom 1:29ff. According to Paul, people who do such things deserve death. This, however, means that such inner thoughts for him are equal to the actual violation of the law (Rom 1:32). The more intensely the mere ego, which is interested only in itself, strives to act according to the law in order to prove itself just in the sight of God and its fellow humans, the more it counts on itself, strengthens the mere ego, and removes itself from the oneness with God in activity. Paul saw this clearly. He realized that he had been, in our terms, a mere ego when he had striven to act according to the law without knowing anything of Christ, who lived in him. From the viewpoint of the Self-ego, he saw what the mere ego was. He had kept all commandments flawlessly. But for him the only reality had been he himself. Paul discusses that in Romans 7: here the mere ego transforms the law, which in itself is holy, just, and good, into an instrument of sin (self-assertion of the ego). Herein lies the difference between the works of the law and the Christian deed. The former is the work of the mere ego, whereas the latter is the deed of the ego, in which the Self, "Christ within me," is revealed. The Christian deed is, therefore, the deed of the ego, through which Christ acts. The Christian deed is the deed that is born by "Christ in humanity," the deed, therefore, that comes from the Self. The ego is no longer the "mere ego," but the ego of the "Self-ego," the ego, then, that the Self reveals itself to and in which the Self reveals itself.

According to my understanding, this differentiation between "the

12. Translation by S. Yagi.
13. Gideons International Bible.

meritorious achievement" (= "work") and "the deed," that is, between the mere ego and the Self-ego, is of fundamental importance. Without this differentiation one does not understand why Jesus told the young man who flawlessly kept the whole law: "One thing you lack, go, sell everything you have. . . . Then come, follow me" (Mark 10:21). In the New Testament there are two views on sin. The one is that of not keeping the law, the other is that everything which originates in the mere ego is sin, because this transforms all gifts of God into an instrument of ego-centeredness (cf. Rom 14:23b).

In the last section, I would like to show how our Self-ego structure of the body corresponds to the teaching of Ueda's dual world.

Dual World and "Self-Ego"

According to Heidegger, human existence is "being in the world" and the being of existence is "worry." But how does worry as the being of existence correlate with the word of Jesus: "Do not worry about your life" (Matt 6:25)? Ueda understands the worry of existence in the world as the concern of the ego. Indeed, it is a fundamental function of the ego to imagine in a given situation the possible alternatives and choose between them. This, however, is based on worry for oneself. Worry for oneself only is a trait of the ego or, in our terms, of the "mere ego." Basically, the ego is insecure. Every ego knows that its being, its position, and its power, along with other aspects of "possessing," are uncertain. The mere ego, however, is worried only about itself and is overwhelmed by this worry. It does not want to gain for itself security that passes, but security that lasts, and this desire is the basis of egoism and egocentrism. We saw above how the mere ego transforms the law, which is good and holy, into a means for one's own security before God and fellow humans.

The world and, therefore, also humans in the world are, according to Ueda, in the "Topos," that is, in the "sphere" of the *śunyatā*, the infinite openness. In this "sphere" the Dharma permeates both the world and the human body. The Dharma bears everything and puts it into mutual relations. This world that is permeated by the Dharma is the home of the Buddha nature or, as the Buddhists call it, the "formless Self," the transindividuum.

The ego as "being-in-the-world" usually does not know about this. But when the "formless Self" reveals itself to and in the ego so that the ego is awakened to it, the whole existence of humanity will be born by the Dharma. In that case, a human being knows the depth that breaks through the worldliness, and one will be relieved from the worldly "merely self-centered worry." A person leads a life in *mushin,* that is, without self-interest and without worry. This is not only Ueda's teaching, but the general Zen teaching. Ueda coined the philosophical term "dual world." That means that we have to differentiate between the worry of the mere ego for itself, and the life without worry of the person that has been awakened. For the mere ego Jesus' words "Do not worry" do not make sense. In general, the words of Jesus are meaningless for the mere ego. The source of Jesus' words is the Self. As "Self-ego" he reveals how the "Self" works in humanity. The so-called ethic of Jesus is not really an ethic, but the simple testimony of the "oneness of divine-human activities," as is the case with all of his words.

The being of the transindividuum is, according to Ueda, the "being in the Topos." Thus the "dual world" is the place of the Self-ego. For in itself, the being of humanity in the world defines the place of the mere ego in the world. The being of the world *and* of humanity in the "Topos," on the other hand, defines the place of the "Individuum qua Transindividuum" (in our terms, Self-ego). In awakening to the dual world, a human is transformed into the "Individuum qua Trans-individuum," and the transindividuum is revealed to and in the ego. In our terms: a human is transformed into the Self-ego. In order to translate this into Christian terms we only have to replace "Dharma" with "Logos" and "Topos" with "God."

In this sense, Ueda's "dual world" is the same as the Christian statement that humanity is in the world and the world is in God. Because the world is in God it is no longer merely world, but becomes creation and God's gift. In Buddhist terms this means that the world is actually the "Land of Buddha." Humans act in a way that — in Christian terms — the reign of God in history, or — according to Buddhist teaching — the Buddhahood of the world, is brought to light.

Both religions meet at the point where reality as it is reveals itself through the thick veil of the mere world. The depth is revealed. A human is not mere ego, but body as Self-ego. The Self is the center of the body, and because of that one can say that awakening is the regaining of the possibilities to realize the body in its wholeness.

If we compare the body with a ship, then the Self is something like the captain and the ego is the helmsman. As the captain of the ship represents the shipping firm, so does the Self in the body represent the transcendence. Actually, the whole body is the unity of the divine and the human, whereas the Self as the center of the body is the place whence this becomes known to the ego. The mere ego, on the other hand, degrades the body to a mere "physical clay," in Paul's words, "flesh," because the mere ego changes the body and the world into a means, mere material that it wants to manipulate.

What the body really is, however, is revealed to the ego when the Self becomes known to and in the ego. Then depth becomes revealed. This depth is the common center of Christians and Buddhists. That this depth really exists is what I wanted to demonstrate on the basis of my dialogue with Buddhists. But why, exactly, because of this dialogue? The dialogue with Buddhists is about the core fact that shows that the Christian religion is not empty belief even in this present situation, but a message that represents and proclaims a reality that can be experienced and can be understood. Both religions testify to this reality, and — as is written — "the testimony of two witnesses is valid" (John 8:17).

IN THOSE DAYS A DECREE WAS ISSUED BY THE EMPEROR AUGUSTUS . . . : THREE CONTEXTUAL BIBLE STUDIES ON LUKE 2

A STAR ILLUMINATES THE DARKNESS

Elsa Tamez

In the middle of the night, in an open field, Luke says that a light shone around some shepherds who lived outside and were keeping watch, by turns, over their flocks (Luke 2:8). Angels announced the glory of God, a gospel, the good news of peace and justice.

One of the greatest preoccupations today in Latin America is violence, the violence of war, in the streets, and in the home. In Colombia more than thirty thousand people die each year, be it from war, domestic violence, criminals, or traffic accidents. It is said that in El Salvador there is very little difference between the deaths that were produced by war and the deaths produced by the violence generated by poverty and unemployment.[1] Domestic violence has intensified in the countries of Latin America so that 30 percent of women in countries like Nicaragua and Peru are beaten or assaulted.[2] The so-called unintentional effects of the free market are generating a globalized violence in all of Latin America. We need to go to the biblical text to search for words of wisdom, peace, and justice for this situation.

I am going to reread Luke 2:1-20 from the context of violence in our midst, with the intention of collaborating with the Bible in the process of creating a culture of peace. I will leave in suspense exegetical problems with respect to form criticism and redaction, as well as the

1. Data presented at the meeting of the Life and Peace Institute held November 9-10, 2000, in Costa Rica.

2. See more data in *Progress of the World's Women,* UNIFEM Biennial Report, 97.

problems of dating the census. I will concentrate more on the sense of the text and its relation to violence and peace. I will orient myself with the questions: When did the good news appear? What is the good news? How is this good news given? And who were the first persons addressed?

Context of the Text and of the Original Readers

Luke wrote his Gospel in a situation filled with conflict: the city of Jerusalem with its temple had been destroyed by the Roman army. Indeed, the whole first century was full of conflict. On different occasions, different movements rose up to challenge the Roman Empire, especially in Galilee, where Jesus began his movement.[3] The dissatisfaction was principally related to the heavy burden of taxes that had to be paid to the Roman treasury and also related to the situation of poverty and injustice that the peasants were suffering.

The author of the Gospel prepared this text in a way that would get the attention not only of his original readers, but also of us, who live in similar situations. The account in Luke 2:1-20 places the birth historically by alluding to the census, to which all provinces had to submit (Luke 2:1-5). He wants his readers to bear in mind the Roman Empire, its apparent peace, and the imposition of the taxes that all had to pay to the emperor.

The census seems to have generated a rebellion in Galilee led by Judas of Galilee.[4] Certainly, according to ancient history, the rebellion led by Judas of Galilee was horribly crushed. The city of Sepphoris, which was some four kilometers from Nazareth, was destroyed in 4 BCE. This is the context in which the narrative of Jesus' birth occurred

3. R. A. Horsley, *Jesus and the Spiral of Violence: Popular Resistance in Roman Palestine* (Minneapolis: Fortress, 1993).

4. Curiously Luke speaks of this rebellion in Acts 5:37. We know from other sources that there is no correspondence between the date of Jesus' birth and the census of Quirinius. Quirinius governed in Syria from 6 to 9 CE. This is not important here. We are looking at Luke's vision with respect to the information he presents and the birth narrative.

and that Luke wants to bring out. Of the twenty verses, five are dedicated to the census and Joseph and Mary's forced journey to register.

The Peace of Augustus Caesar
and the Peace of Jesus of Nazareth

Luke seems to be interested in describing the announcement of Jesus as a new alternative of peace, when faced with the suffering of the Jewish people, caused by the Roman Empire and the local allied governments.

According to Luke, an angel appears to the shepherds during the night and says to them, "Do not be afraid: for see — I am bringing you good news of great joy for all the people: to you is born this day in the city of David a Savior, who is the Messiah, the Lord." In the churches, we usually read these titles of Jesus as belonging to Christology and separate from their context. Nevertheless, behind these titles, the figure of Augustus is deliberately evoked,[5] because everyone knew that Augustus was known as the *sōtēr,* the "savior"; and that the Greek word *euangelizō,* "announce good news," was used to announce the decrees or important happenings of the emperor. Also the word *kyrios,* "Lord," was a title used for the emperor. *Kyrios* is the title that was assigned to Jesus after the resurrection, but Luke places it before Jesus' own birth. So then, we agree with Herman Hendrickx that it is not accidental that in the birth narrative, Jesus is seen as the true Savior, Lord, and one who brings peace. Augustus was famous for his peace; peace and harmony were the slogans of the empire. According to the ancient historians, with the triumph of Augustus over Mark Antony, the era of peace began. Augustus stopped the civil wars and imposed peace in all the provinces. To contrast the peace of Jesus Christ with the peace of the empire, Luke describes an army of angels singing: "Glory to God in the highest heaven, and on earth peace among those whom God favors!" (v. 14). For Luke, Jesus is the fulfillment of the messianic promises of peace. He is the Messiah, the most

---

5. Cf. Herman Hendrickx, *The Third Gospel for the Third World,* vol. 1: *Preface and Infancy Narrative (Luke 1:1–2:52)* (Collegeville, Minn.: Liturgical Press, 1996), 197.

hoped-for figure for the Jews in those conflictive times, to liberate the people from the Roman occupation.

There is, then, in this text a deliberate description of Jesus, similar to that of Caesar,[6] but with the intention not of exalting the child but of contrasting him with Caesar. Luke gives us to understand that the true peace does not come from the empire but from Jesus of Nazareth, the son of Mary and Joseph. Even if it is certain that the two figures are similar, a great difference separates them: the condition of poverty surrounding Jesus' birth and the first announcement being to the shepherds.

The repeated mention of the place where the child was born (3 times) and this being considered as a sign (*sēmeion*) distance it from the powerful emperor. Mary wrapped Jesus in bands of cloth and laid him in a manger. The manger was a place where animals ate. The story tells us that they did not find a place in the inn (*katalyma,* a humble place where travelers passed the night, or a room in a peasant's house, not a *pandocheion,* "hotel"). They were only able to find a place in a stable or in a place where poor peasants put their animals. It is said that the peasants' houses were generally just one room. The people slept on one side and the animals on the other; in the middle was the manger.[7] It was there, in this place, that Mary laid her son, whom Luke calls Savior, Messiah, and Lord. He repeats it three times. Luke's Savior is poor, and the angels see this as a sign, which gives the shepherds great joy, for they are also poor.

Against all messianic expectations of his time that hoped for a great military leader who would confront the Roman Empire with his army, Luke describes the Messiah as a vulnerable child, wrapped in bands of cloth, of humble origins. The peace that Luke has in mind is not the Pax Romana that uses armies to conquer other peoples in order to exploit them.[8] It is the fulfillment of the messianic promises of peace and goodwill, the *shalom* of the Hebrew Scriptures.

6. Cf. the inscription of Priene and others.

7. Hendrickx, *Gospel,* 183.

8. K. Wengst, *Pax Romana and the Peace of Jesus Christ* (Philadelphia: Fortress, 1987).

To Whom Is the Good News Announced?

Within the structure of the text, it is curious to observe that Luke dedicates five verses to the census, two verses to the birth narrative, and thirteen verses to the shepherds. Obviously, looking to the receivers of the good news is more important for Luke. These are the shepherds. The text says that they lived out in the open and took turns watching over the flocks of sheep. The majority of commentators affirm their poverty and humble conditions.[9] The light shone first on the shepherds; they were chosen to be the first to receive the good news of peace that was initiated by the birth of Jesus. In this sense, it was announced first to those who suffered most under the Pax Romana: the poor. The shepherds are the representatives of all poor people. This news will bring great joy to them, says the angel, and also to all the people in general (v. 10).

The strange sign given by the angel, to find a child wrapped in bands of cloth and lying in a manger, intensifies the shepherds' joy, because they see in the Messiah someone in their same condition. The sign gives happiness not only to the shepherds but also to the host of angels that from heaven announce the glory of God in the highest, and on earth peace among those whom God favors,[10] which are those who have suffered most the consequences of the "peace" of Augustus.

The story continues. The shepherds go to see the sign, tell Mary and Joseph what had happened, and all who were there were amazed at what they heard. It seems that the "evangelized" shepherds became the "evangelizers."

---

9. Cf., in loc., J. A. Fitzmyer, *Gospel According to Luke I–IX,* Anchor Bible (Garden City, N.Y.: Doubleday, 1981); D. Bock, *Luke 1:1–9:50* (Grand Rapids: Baker, 1994); C. E. Freire, *Devolver el Evangelio a los pobres* (Salamanca: Sigueme, 1978), 294-301; Hendrickx, *Gospel.*

10. We adopt the reading *eudokias,* which is documented best, and understand the genitive as (to those) "whom he favors."

The Message of Christmas to the Churches

Today we live Christmas as a truce, that is, a temporary suspension of hostilities, a passing "cease fire." As the days pass, the struggle for survival in the cities and the countryside continues, the violence of the street rises; in the places where there is armed conflict, the guerrillas and the army resume the war. The Christmas lights are pretty but do not last long, nor do the fireworks. As the days pass, people wake up as if from a dream, and return to their routine, in debt, to suffer or to be a witness of the daily injustices and violence that is now installed as part of the culture. Only triumphant commerce sits to count their profit. It is not true that in Latin America we have peace after the end of the dictatorships. The culture of the market is a culture of war for survival.

In the Gospel of Luke we find the narration of the nativity as the proposal of a beginning of a new life, opposite of that lived in that time, a proposal of peace and justice for all men and women, beginning with the least favored of society. Let us make the proposal of Luke our own and receive Christmas as the fulfillment of the messianic promises of peace.

THE STORY OF JESUS' BIRTH (LUKE 1–2): AN AFRICAN READING

Justin Ukpong

In this essay I shall read Luke's story of Jesus' birth (Luke 1 and 2) against an African contemporary context focusing on its socio-historical dimension, and shall use the methodology of inculturation hermeneutics. I shall especially stress the strong political, social, economic, and religious implications of this narrative.

Contemporary African Context of the Reading

In recent years, the sociopolitical problems of Africa that had been expected to diminish as the years went by have rather alarmingly escalated. Standing out as a sore thumb among these is the Tutsi-Hutu ethnic conflict in Rwanda that started in 1994 and has not yet totally healed. At the core of the conflict lies the thirst for political power and supremacy in the country. In order to stay on in power, those who have access to it seek to eliminate the others within the same country along ethnic lines. In South Africa, while the apartheid that brought about the suppression of the majority of the population by a small minority has crumbled, its social, psychological, and economic effects still lurk around, evidence of which is the malnourished street children and the violence one encounters in that country. In western Africa, while Liberia and Sierra Leone are licking the wounds of long-drawn-out civil wars, a new conflict has erupted in that otherwise peaceful country, Ivory Coast. Again, it is about political power and its illegitimate use to suppress people. In the northern horn of the continent, while Eritrea may be experiencing an uneasy calm, the Sudan seems to be in a perpetual state of war as those who acquire political power use it to suppress people along religious lines. In the 1990s, people looked forward to the twenty-first century with great expectation of political and economic renewal for Africa, but events have belied that dream.

The United Nations Development Program (UNDP) has ranked Africa lowest in terms of achieving development goals. Poverty marks the life of the majority of the population. In many countries the unemployment rate has for long stayed in double digits, adding fuel to such other endemic ills as bribery and corruption of different kinds. The IMF and the World Bank have not helped matters; rather they have added to the economic woes of African nations with the introduction of the Economic Structural Adjustment Program (ESAP) in the Third World in the last two decades. The program includes the devaluation of national currencies, removal of government protection on international trade and the national economy, removal of subsidies on essential commodities, introduction of certain features of a highly capitalist consumer culture like sales tax, and so on. This program undertaken in the name of globalization has worked adversely for the economy of African nations because it involves the integration of the weak economies of Africa into the stronger economies of the West.

In both the political and economic situations, those that bear the brunt of the suffering are the common people, the poor, women, and children. The common people in Africa today are going through severe economic and political tensions. Political and economic power is being wielded to their great disadvantage. What is the significance of Luke's story of Jesus' birth in such a situation?

Textual Analysis of Luke 1:5–2:40

Background of Luke's Story

It is generally accepted that Luke's Gospel was written about 70-80 CE for a predominantly Gentile church outside Palestine, possibly Antioch in Syria. This was in the aftermath of the First Jewish War, in which the Roman rule in Palestine showed its might in crushing the Jewish revolt and in the destruction of the Jerusalem temple. This event, along with the expulsion of Christians from the synagogue and the temple around the same period, and state persecution of Christians, would have raised religious and political questions for Christians of Luke's community. The religious question had to do with the group's relationship to Judaism: Was the Jesus movement to remain a sect of Judaism or have its independent existence? What was its position in relation to Judaism? In view of the fact that first-century CE Palestine had witnessed revolutionary movements that were crushed, like that of the Zealots, the political question would have been about the situation of the Jesus movement under a repressive colonial rule: What future did the Jesus movement have under such a situation? How was it different from the other movements? Luke's Gospel shows evidence of an attempt to grapple with these issues.

Luke's interest in Jesus' Davidic descent (1:27, 32; 3:23-38), the association of Jesus with the aristocracy through Zechariah the priest (1:5, 36), and the tracing of Jesus' genealogy to Adam (3:23-38) betray an attempt to answer the religious question in the story of Jesus' birth and early life. All this seems to say that Jesus, the founder of Christianity, is genealogically a true representative of royal Jewish stock, and of all of humanity; thus Christianity is rooted in Judaism yet at the same time open to all peoples. Put differently, though Jesus is born with the credentials of a Davidic king, he is for all peoples, and hence the Jesus movement is for all peoples.[1]

---

1. W. M. Swartley, "Politics or Peace *(Eirēnē)* in Luke's Gospel," in R. J. Cassidy and P. J. Scharper, eds., *Political Issues in Luke-Acts* (Maryknoll, N.Y.: Orbis, 1983), 33.

Hans Conzelmann has appraised Luke's Gospel as having no critical stance toward the political presence of Rome in Palestine. He sees Luke as preoccupied with showing the continuity of Christianity with Judaism and at the same time distancing it from Judaism in its political import to put Christianity in a favorable light in the empire. He therefore paints an apolitical image of the Lukan Jesus.[2] John Yoder and Richard Cassidy have contested Conzelmann's view of Luke's political apologetic.[3] Both see the Lukan Jesus as socially and politically revolutionary, though not constituting the same kind of threat to the Roman rule as the Zealots and the Parthians. Jesus' revolution was not about the overthrow of the Romans, as was the Zealots', or the formation of an alternative home-grown government. Rather, it was about a radically new social pattern of living, a radical transformation in the configuration of the contemporary religious, political, social, and economic relations as shown in his interest in the poor and the marginalized people in society, and his criticism of the rich (Luke 1:53; 6:24; 16:19; 21:1). Certainly if a large enough number of people followed his way long enough, the movement could ultimately be a threat to Roman rule.

In a sense, both positions are founded on the Lukan text — Luke himself has contributed to the confusion. The confusion arises because Luke espouses an upper/middle-class ideology while drawing from the resources of the lower class. Therefore, one who follows Luke's ideological position is bound to root for an apolitical Lukan Jesus; but quarrying from the lower-class material and reading the text against the grain yields a different image — a revolutionary Jesus. To be sure, Luke himself is obviously interested in the marginalized people in society: women who were at the fringe of the social circle, the poor, tax collectors, and sinners. The combination of an upper-class ideology with a keen interest in the poor constitutes Luke's way of responding to the

---

2. H. Conzelmann, *The Theology of St. Luke* (New York: Harper & Row, 1961), 138-48.

3. J. H. Yoder, *The Politics of Jesus* (Grand Rapids: Eerdmans, 1972), 26-67; R. J. Cassidy, *Jesus, Politics, and Society: A Study of Luke's Gospel* (Maryknoll, N.Y.: Orbis, 1978), 20-49, 50-59.

political question. Luke seems to be telling the middle/upper class and the elite that the Jesus movement is different from the other movements — it is interested in the poor, not in the overthrow of Rome. In that way an impression is created that this is not a politically dangerous movement in view of its "open door" policy. When the text is read against the grain, however, in spite of himself Luke gives us the very facts that reveal the movement's revolutionary potential.

Our guiding question is: What does the birth story say of Jesus' person and mission in the face of the mighty power of Rome? The hermeneutical question is: How does Luke's story inspire, encourage, and empower the politically and economically oppressed and powerless today? In view of Luke's upper-class ideological stance vis-à-vis his interest in the poor, it is only through reading between the lines, as indicated above, that the text can be expected to reveal its true liberating power.[4]

My thesis is: Luke's narrative of the birth of Jesus has one central theme that returns in each scene of the whole story. That theme is that *in the coming of Jesus God has raised up the weak and the lowly, and simultaneously put down the great and the mighty* (this means that both parties now exist as equals as God created them and meant them to be). There is a message of hope for the weak, the lowly, and the oppressed in the birth narrative.

Announcement of John's Conception, 1:5-25

Luke prefaces the story of Jesus' birth with that of John the Baptist, which is another birth through divine revelation. Luke's political and religious consciousness shows up in his reference to Herod as the political ruler at the time, mention of the temple as the locus of the revelation, and the priestly lineage of Zechariah and Elizabeth.

Luke tells us that Zechariah was a priest. This means that he belonged to the aristocracy. When he learns of the coming birth of John,

4. J. I. Mosala, *Biblical Hermeneutics and Black Theology in South Africa* (Grand Rapids: Eerdmans, 1989), 176-78, here 186.

who was to prepare the way for Jesus, Zechariah is rendered mute (possibly deaf too). This makes him unable to function in his aristocratic position for some time. Deaf-mutes were objects of pity in society; they were not fully integrated into society and were counted among the outcast. Albeit temporarily, Zechariah shared the lot of the outcast, people on the margin of society, to symbolize what John and Jesus stood for.

Announcement of Jesus' Conception, 1:26-38

The announcement of Jesus' conception is made to Mary by Gabriel, the same angel that announced the conception of John. Gabriel informs Mary that by the power of the Holy Spirit (without human intercourse) she would conceive and bear the Son of God. Her son's name was to be *Yeshua* (i.e., Jesus), which means "Yahweh saves/Yahweh is liberator/Yahweh is liberation." God will give him the throne of David his ancestor and he will rule over Israel forever. Behind these words of the angel lies the Jewish expectation of *the* messianic king who would liberate and rule Israel forever in justice and peace. The angel therefore designates Jesus as the messianic king that the people were expecting.

Research on the social conditions of Palestine at the time of Jesus reveals that political oppression went hand in hand with economic oppression. There existed a threefold social structure: the nobility and those who belonged to the economic and political ruling classes; those who belonged to the lower classes, the poor, artisans, lower-stratum priests, peasants; and those who belonged to the underclasses — casual laborers, prostitutes, criminals, beggars.[5] Joseph's profession (artisan/carpenter) indicates that he belonged to the lower class of society, and Mary's betrothal to him indicates her belonging there too. The fulfillment of the angel's announcement to Mary would mean her conceiving outside wedlock, a shameful thing that would put her in an even more marginal position in society. The event itself took place in Naza-

5. M. Clevenot, *Materialist Approaches to the Bible* (Maryknoll, N.Y.: Orbis, 1985), 50; S. Freyne, *Galilee, Jesus and the Gospels: Literary Approaches and Historical Investigations* (Philadelphia: Fortress, 1988), 156-58.

reth, a small town of about two hundred people in Galilee,[6] "a province scorned as a secondary outpost of Judaism."[7] It was also geographically and politically on the margin. Nazareth, the home of Mary, Joseph, and the would-be Messiah, was therefore in every respect a marginal town from where, proverbially, nothing good could come (John 1:46).

The messianic king and liberator was then to be part of the poor and the lowly. These are the ones that need liberation; it is from among them that the liberator comes. The rich and the oppressors would also be liberated from their practice of exploitation but only through solidarity with the poor.

Visit to Elizabeth, 1:39-56

By means of the meeting of Elizabeth and Mary, Luke shows that in God's plan John's conception was in view of Jesus' conception. Thus it was in view of the coming of Jesus that Zechariah and Elizabeth, who had longed for children all their lives and suffered the ignominy that went with the misfortune of childlessness in that society, were blessed with a son in their old age. In other words, right from the beginning Jesus' coming is associated with taking away the reproach of people. The two songs of praise by the two women that follow further articulate this.

Elizabeth's canticle, less well known than Mary's Magnificat, and likely a Lukan composition, focuses on the would-be mother of the Messiah, and is no less a praise of God who raises up the weak and the lowly than the Magnificat is. The opening words, "Blessed are you among women," echo Old Testament words about Jael (Judg 5:24) and Judith (Jdt 13:18). God had used these women to overcome the mighty enemies of Israel. Mary is here identified with them, that is, she is put in the same liberating category as they.

6. J. D. Crossan, *Jesus: A Revolutionary Biography* (San Francisco: HarperCollins, 1994), 26.

7. J. Kodell, "Luke," in D. Bergant and R. J. Karris, eds., *The Collegeville Bible Commentary* (Collegeville, Minn.: Liturgical Press, 1989), 940.

The Magnificat (1:46-55), a pre-Lukan hymn of the 'anawim, the poor of Yahweh,[8] proclaims God as one who lifts up the poor and the lowly, bringing down the rich and the mighty in the process. It echoes the songs of Hannah (1 Sam 2:1-10) and Judith (Jdt 13:18; 16:11). It is put on Mary's lips by Luke as a commentary on God's action in the unexpected choice of Mary, a poor rural girl, to be the mother of the long-awaited Messiah (1:46-49). The hymn has political, economic, and religious revolutionary overtones. God's action in Mary is seen as "part of a long-standing process of overthrowing proud human expectations and exalting the lowly."[9] In Mary, God has turned things upside down.

Birth of John, 1:57-80

After John's birth, on the occasion of his circumcision and naming, his father Zechariah regained his power of speech and praised God with a hymn. The hymn, the Benedictus, most likely a combination of two pre-Lukan hymns,[10] is placed on the lips of Zechariah as a commentary on John's birth. The birth marks the definitive arrival of divine salvation long hoped for — the overthrow of enemies, forgiveness of sin, peace, and light to the Gentiles who are in darkness. John's role is to prepare the people to receive God's salvation.

Birth of Jesus, 2:1-7

The messianic overtones in the angel's announcement cannot be missed. There is an echo of Isaiah 9:6, "For unto us a child is born, unto us a son is given." The child was to be of David's royal house, and Jesus was. The angel brought "good news" meant for all people (laos), not

---

8. R. E. Brown, *The Birth of the Messiah* (New York: Doubleday, 1993), 350-54; R. J. Karris, "The Gospel According to Luke," in R. E. Brown, J. A. Fitzmyer, and R. E. Murphy, eds., *The New Jerome Biblical Commentary* (New York: Prentice-Hall, 1990), 681.

9. Kodell, "Luke," 941.

10. H. Schürmann, *Das Lukasevangelium*, Herders Theologischer Kommentar zum Neuen Testament 3/1 (Freiburg im Breisgau: Herder, 1969), 84-94.

just for the Jews (2:10). Jesus' birth is good news to people everywhere but especially for the shepherds, the poor and the marginalized. It is a fulfillment of the Old Testament messianic prophecies. This is a foreshadowing of Luke 4:16-19, where the mission of Jesus is clarified in terms of Isaiah's messianic message of restoration for the marginalized in society and bringing the good news to the poor.

Like the story of the annunciation to Zechariah, Luke's story of the birth of Jesus is set within a political context — with a reference to the census of Quirinius. Historical research has, however, shown Luke's chronology to be inaccurate and inconsistent in locating Jesus' birth during Quirinius's census (2:1-3), which took place about 6-7 CE.[11] It seems Jesus was born about 3 BCE, ten years before Quirinius's census.[12] In any case the story of Jesus' birth is to be read against the backdrop of the political atmosphere of 4 BCE–7 CE in Palestine, a period of great political repression and subjugation in the history of Palestine. Historically it is known that the death of Herod the Great in 4 BCE brought about a great revolt among the peasants in the whole country. This revolt was severely crushed by the Syrian governor Publius Quinctilius Varus, and Roman domination was securely reestablished. Similarly, Quirinius's census, which was for purposes of taxation, occasioned a revolt led by Judas the Galilean. The rebellion was again quickly crushed and Judas was executed.[13]

Historical research has shown the unlikelihood of Joseph and Mary being required to make a journey from Nazareth to Bethlehem for a census.[14] Therefore, this part of the story must be understood in terms of the theological significance it serves. That Joseph and Mary had to make a trip to Bethlehem for a census, for one thing, points to the social and economic stress that politically subjugated people had to undergo. For another, it has a theological value as a fulfillment of the

11. Brown, *Birth*, 548.

12. R. Syme, "The Titulus Tiburtinus," in *Akten des 6. Internationalen Kongresses für griechische und lateinische Epigraphik,* Vestigia. Beiträge zur Alten Geschichte 17 (Munich: Beck, 1973), 585-601.

13. Brown, *Birth*, 413; Crossan, *Jesus*, 21-22; Syme, "Titulus," 600.

14. Brown, *Birth*, 549.

Old Testament prophecy that the Messiah would be born in Bethlehem (Mic 5:1-3). Birth in a manger highlights the lowly circumstance of this event and Jesus' solidarity with the poor and the lowly right from his birth. This is further heightened by the fact that the first to receive the official announcement of the birth and to visit the baby were shepherds. In Jesus' time, many considered shepherds to be dishonest people because they often grazed their flocks on other people's lands. They were considered to be outside the law and unclean. They belonged to the lower rung of the social ladder.[15] Thus it is nonentities in society who were the first to be chosen as official beneficiaries of the good news of God's salvation to the world. Jesus' birth is for the liberation of such people.

The event occasioned the angelic hymn, the Gloria. This is likely a composition of early Jewish Christians used here by Luke in a christological context. It announces that the glory of God is revealed in the coming of Jesus, and the effect of this is peace *(eirēnē)* on earth. "Peace" here embodies the multifaceted uses of *shalom* in the Old Testament that include well-being, salvation, justice, faithfulness, love, and so on. It is in the service of God's will, to make things new, to restore all things — religious, political, social, economic — in society.[16] The shepherds clearly belong to those favored with the peace of God, Mary occupying the prime position (Luke 1:28). The birth of Jesus thus means that the time of God's favor on the poor, the marginalized, the politically subjugated, and the oppressed has arrived.

Significance of Luke's Story of Jesus' Birth

The birth of Jesus was a political threat to the oppressive Roman government in Palestine. In Luke one has to read between the lines to get

---

15. F. W. Danker, *Jesus and the New Age According to St. Luke* (St. Louis: Clayton, 1972), 72.

16. Swartley, "Politics," 34; I. H. Marshall, *Luke: Historian and Theologian* (Grand Rapids: Zondervan, 1970), 97-102.

this — he presents it covertly and subtly. As Luke presents it, we have here the story of God's intervention on behalf of the poor and the lowly to raise them up, give them a new hope, and empower them to struggle for equality and justice in society. God's people had learned that empires rise and fall. Might not the birth of Jesus be the definitive intervention of God to bring down the ruling Roman Empire and bring liberation to the oppressed? By the same token, might not the birth of Jesus spell liberation for the politically, socially, and economically oppressed common people in Africa today?

For the common people in Africa, the story of Jesus' birth is a message of hope. As happened in the ancient world, they have watched repressive regimes in their continent fall one after another; they have seen mighty rulers, who thought they had no need of God or the common people, topple. Attainment of political independence in Africa in the mid-twentieth century meant the fall of colonialism and the rise of democratic self-rule in that continent. In South Africa the demise of the apartheid system in 1994 meant the rise of the democratic process for the common people of that nation. All this has been the work of God. Today political strife and violence bedevil the continent everywhere. Political oppression goes hand in hand with economic deprivation, injustice, bribery, different forms of corruption, neglect of the social system whereby the poor could get economic relief, and so on. All these come through a systemic suppression of the poor and the voiceless. Will the God that mightily did great things in the past not do the same today? Might not the same God in Jesus liberate the lowly and the oppressed as the mighty people that oppress them get brought down? The message of the story is that the way God consistently operates gives the assurance that this will be so.

As pointed out above, the basic theme of Luke's story of the birth of Jesus is that in the coming of Jesus God has raised up the weak and the lowly, an action that simultaneously puts down the great and the mighty such that both parties now exist as equals (as God created them and meant them to be). Raising up the lowly means breaking down the bond of oppression by the mighty that subjugates the lowly. It is indeed good news, a message of hope for the weak, the lowly, and the oppressed. Read against the background of the current political and economic situation in Africa, the Christmas story holds out hope and reassurance for the common people.

MARY AND MAYA

Seiichi Yagi

It is not an easy task to interpret the Christmas story in the Japanese context, and I want to do it in the light of the Buddhist-Christian dialogue.[1]

Buddhists, too, tell the story of the miraculous birth of their saint, Gautama Buddha. This tale has an ancient tradition, which reached its last stage of development in the Buddhist text "Gaṇḍavyūha." It is one part of the "Avataṃsaka-Sūtra," which originated most probably in the fourth century in Central Asia. This Sutra is made up of different writings that are actually independent from one another, but as a whole they contain the story of the awakened Buddha. "Gaṇḍavyūha," the eighth lecture, talks about a boy, Sudhana, who visited fifty-three saints and asked each of them about the truth. "Gaṇḍavyūha" is, therefore, also called "entrance into the world of truth" or "pilgrimage to the enlightenment."

On his pilgrimage the boy Sudhana sees Māyā Devī, the mother of Gautama Buddha and wife of King Suddhōdana. The boy really wants to meet her, and while he thinks of a way to achieve his goal a goddess appears and asks him to purify the citadel of his heart. Soon many gods appear, and one of them throws the net of lights over the boy. The net sinks into his body and enables him to see the Buddha of birth, Māyā. In an intense meditation the boy sees a big lotus flower made of gemstones rising from the earth. On top of this lotus flower

---

1. I owe the subject and the Buddhist material to E. Kobayashi, "Mary and Maya, Two Holy Wombs," paper at the 18th Congress of the Tozai Shukyo Koryu Gakkai, 25 July 2000.

stands a palace, and in the center on a lotus armchair made of the gem-stone Mani there sits Maya Devi. The Sutra uses imaginative language to show how within her all the religious virtues, powers, and beauties are embodied. The boy puts a question to Māyā: How do the bodhisat-tvas[2] exercise their practice and obtain perfect wisdom? Queen Māyā replies and tells him who she is and what she can show him. In "Gandavyūha" she is not a historical person, but her name, Māyā, sug-gests that she is a heavenly universal being. (Literally, *māyā* means illu-sion; in Buddhist thought it means ever-changing beauty, but also nonsubstantiality, that is, *śūnyatā* [void], and superworldly wisdom as the ground of the Buddhahood.) Māyā explains that she took a vow in the presence of a Buddha to become the mother of all Buddhas. This vow was fulfilled so that she really became mother of all Buddhas and bodhisattvas. Therefore, Māyā in "Gaṇḍavyūha" is the uterus of all Buddhas, the ground of all Buddhahood.

Māyā continues her story and tells the boy that the birth of Gautama Buddha was something extraordinary. A bodhisattva, in fact the preexistent Gautama Buddha, radiated lights from all pores of his body. These lights fell on all pores of Māyā Devī's body and penetrated it. The womb of Māyā Devī received all these lights and together with them it received all bodhisattvas and all saints. Gautama Buddha was then born out of her right side. When she finished her story Māyā told the boy pilgrim that she was able to tell him only about her vow and its fulfillment. If he wanted to know more he should go to the other saints.

We notice here a striking similarity to Luke 1 and 2: there is some-thing miraculous about the birth of Jesus and of Gautama. Māyā Devī, King Suddhodana's wife, was not a virgin. But we read that the king was not involved in his wife's pregnancy. That Gautama was born out of his mother's right side emphasizes the immaculateness[3] of mother and child more strongly than does the story in Luke, which only tells about Mary's virginal conception. As a matter of fact, the early "Mahāyānā" bi-

2. The candidates to the Buddhahood.

3. In some old Indian epics the heroes are born out of the right side of the mother. In this case, that shows their supernatural power.

ography of Buddha, "Lalitavistara" (3rd century), was written in order to convince the people of the immaculateness of Gautama and Māyā. "Lalitavistara" has a strong tendency toward the glorification of Buddha and tells another version of Gautama Buddha's supernatural birth.

No doubt, there are also differences. While Luke stands at the beginning of a development toward Mariology, "Gaṇḍavyūha" deals with the final stage in the glorification of Māyā. Because of this, the narrative style of "Gaṇḍavyūha" is imaginative. The story makes use of magnificent symbols and is full of supernatural, wonderful characters and events. Luke 2 is much simpler and more realistic despite the fact that Luke, too, talks about the wonderful. Māyā was queen and gave birth to Gautama in the palace. Mary was a virgin and came from a small town called Nazareth. Jesus was placed in a manger, and so on. Also important is that whereas the shepherds were allowed to approach the holy family without restrictions, the boy, Sudhana, had to purify himself first and be endowed with all sorts of virtues in order to be able to see Māyā. The distance from the everyday human being is much greater in the case of Māyā than in Mary's case, even with the glorified Mary. The reason for that is that Māyā, as the ground of the Buddhahood, is a universal being. Humans have to be awakened to it themselves in order to be able to see her.

Herein lies the biggest difference between Mary and Māyā. The context of the Buddhist story is the pilgrimage of a boy to awakening. The essential question is how a person can reach awakening. The boy Sudhana asks about the truth. Before Māyā appears to him his heart is purified and he is endowed with virtues and powers. Before him appears a lotus flower set with precious Maṇi stones, and in the middle of the lotus flower stands a palace in which a lotus-flower armchair made of Maṇi is placed. Māyā sits on it, a heavenly figure, embodying all virtues and all charisma. She tells the boy how she herself took a vow to give birth to Buddhas that was fulfilled. Notice that the lotus flower, the gemstone Maṇi, and so on are all symbols of awakening. Gautama Buddha is actually the teacher of awakening, not a redeemer.

Luke's Gospel is quite different. Luke 1 and 2 deal with history. Joseph is a descendant of David. Jesus is born in the city of David. The angel tells Mary that God would give Jesus the throne of David and that Jesus would reign over the house of Jacob forever (1:32-33). Mary praises the Lord, saying that God would not forget his promise to Israel. He would bring down rulers from their thrones, but would lift up the humble (1:52). Indeed, an angel appears to the shepherds, the lowly, and announces the good news, and the shepherds are the first to "find" the infant Jesus. It is prophesied about John, the son of Zechariah, that he would bring back to the Lord many of the people of Israel (1:16; cf. 1:77). Jesus is "a light for revelation to the Gentiles" (2:32), but it is added at the same time that Jesus is a light for glory to the people of God, Israel.[4] All this probably comes from the Jewish-Christian tradition that Luke adopted. In this reference to the history of salvation lies a characteristic of Christianity that compares to Buddhism.

In the New Testament Jesus Christ is the liberator. He liberates the people from the wrath of God, from the rule of sin, and from all evil powers. In the end he is victorious. "Then the end will come, when he hands over the kingdom to God the Father after he has destroyed all dominion, authority, and power. For he must reign until he has put all his enemies under his feet. The last enemy to be destroyed is death" (1 Cor 15:24-26).

The New Testament, too, deals with awakening. In Rudolf Bultmann's terms, the New Testament shows the way in which one can reach true self-understanding. We can also call it "awakened self-understanding." Even though Bultmann was not aware of it, with his term "self-understanding" he touched a central idea of Buddhism, which is the awakening-to-oneself, in other words, enlightenment. When Paul says that God "made his light shine in our hearts to give us the light of the knowledge of the glory of God in the face of Christ" (2 Cor 4:6), he expresses nothing other than what the Buddhists call enlightenment (according to Akizuki, a famous Zen master). It is the core of Buddhism around which everything else revolves. It can be compared to a circle with a center.

4. All Bible citations are from *The Holy Bible, New International Version* (New York: International Bible Society, 1978).

In contrast to that we can compare Christianity to an ellipse with two foci: history and the awakened self-understanding. In Christianity both are combined. In Luke 1 and 2, or rather in Luke's entire work, only one focus is dominant: history. Is the theme of the awakened self-understanding missing in Luke? To me, it is Luke's understanding of humanity before God that corresponds with the awakened self-understanding: "For everyone who exalts himself will be humbled, and he who humbles himself will be exalted" (Luke 18:14b; cf. 1:51ff.). This is often called "reversal of values." For Jesus this must have been different; worldly differences have no significance before God. "Whoever does God's will is my brother and sister and mother" (Mark 3:35). The theme of the awakened self-understanding is by no means missing in Luke. He just expressed it differently.

What does the Christmas story mean in the present Japanese context? In Japan the gap between the poor and the rich, the low and the powerful, is relatively small. The walls between the different social levels of society are not thick. Over 90 percent of the whole population counts itself as middle class, and the standard of living is quite high. The unemployment rate is reasonably low, although at 4.5 percent it is presently as high as it has never been since the Second World War. As in most Western countries, life expectancy is very high, and almost 50 percent of young people receive higher education. Social unrest is low, and although the crime rate increases the overall security is still very high. The number of women who think of themselves as being discriminated against is small.

Our problem is the total secularization and the economic focus of society. Neither in private nor in public do people care much about transcendence. The infant Jesus, that is, potential religiosity, is pushed out into the cold, and in that sense "lies in the manger." But Luke sees just in this "child lying in the manger" the sign of the glory of God (Luke 2:12-14).

It was an extremely unexpected, extraordinary event that Mary and Māyā received their holy children and gave birth to them. Therefore, we will not give up our faith and hope in the activity of the transcendent.

INSTEAD OF A CONCLUSION:
THEOLOGICAL ASTRONOMY — A PARABLE

Walter Dietrich

Please imagine the scientific theology in the Northern Hemisphere as being a huge astronomical research laboratory, which is subdivided into various segments. We theologians work in innumerable workshops, halls, and observatories: Anglo-American ones; northern, southern, and central European ones; Protestant and Catholic ones; and so on. They contain different offices and research areas, that is, for biblical, historical, systematic, or practical astronomy (to name just a few generic terms). We use a variety of techniques: historical critique, statistics, logic, feminism, computer science, rhetoric, mysticism, aesthetics, and so on. We also get inspiration from the neighboring laboratories: the philosophical, the archeological, the historical, the philological, the sociological, the pedagogical, religious studies, the psychological, the musicological, the aesthetic and art-historical, and so on. We work with very different basic premises and have different aims in mind: more conservative or more progressive, more linked to our confession or more liberal, with more inner involvement or rather distanced and rational, more believing or more doubting.

In short: we are extremely differentiated and tolerant and very busy, sometimes even very creative. Why do we do all that? The answer is obvious: Astronomy is about *star research*. We shall and we want to discover stars above us and study them as closely as possible. Let us consider the Bible. Already here, in this basic book of ours, stars are mentioned over and over again. Remember, for instance, the patriarch Abraham: God asks him to count the stars in the sky, and Abraham cannot accomplish the task; or remember the star of Bethlehem or the iconography of Mary (and already the Mesopotamian goddess Ishtar) in a ring of light, or remember the chorale "Oh Christ, You Precious Morning Star," which goes back to a self-portrait of Christ as the world's judge as we encounter him on the last page of the Bible (Revelation 22).

The question asked in a pious German children's song: "Do you know how many stars there are?" is the cardinal question we astronomers are asked. And if we are honest we will have to answer: No, actually, we do *not* know. We know that stars exist; we know it from children's songs, chorales, Bible verses, paintings, and stories, but we probably do not know it from scientific astronomy. We hear it in ancient words and read it in ancient scripts: up there are stars, many stars, bright stars, brilliant stars. We also know about our mission — to find the stars and show them to people: to students, to members of churches, to people in general. This is, in a nutshell, what the whole workplace is for, anyway: laboratories, shops, halls, "think tanks," observatories, computers and servers, analyses, lectures, books. Yes, we do work busily and are quite productive. Only the "star thing" will not really work.

Sometimes, admittedly, one can hear a shout from one hall or the other: "Here! There! I saw something! I discovered it. Here, an ancient star! There, a brand new one!" Then the star scholars come running, they meet, gesticulate, have discussions, and put their devices and methods to use, and shout: "No, we do it *this way* here. No, you are not at all up to date. No, have you never heard about Umberto Eco and the aesthetics of reception? No, the Holy Father has given different instructions. No, yes, never ever, but yes, in no case." Finally, a huge telescope is put up, and beside it some two to five other ones, just slightly smaller in size, and all of them focus on a similar, but nevertheless noticeably different, direction — and a little later, disillusionment spreads: probably nothing after all! Again: Nothing! Maybe part of a phenomenon, a glimmer of truth, a shooting star, short-lived, not capable of securing a consensus. They realize it, go back to their halls and to their workplaces — that is, most of them have continued their work there anyway and have not been willing to let any sudden commotion interrupt them. This is (and admittedly, I am being very self-critical and maybe after all a little bit unfair, but nevertheless, an overall picture) the state the northern astronomy is in.

Then, one day, something peculiar happens. The Bernese laboratory runs an astronomical symposium and invites three star scholars from far away. It reminds us of a famous story from our ancient books — except that this time only one of these three sages comes from the east, and the others are from the south; and this time they are not all men, but one is a woman. In their home countries these three are highly respected star scholars, even though, unlike us, they do not have well-equipped "think tanks," computers, servers, but rather very modest telescopes and a comparatively limited amount of books.

These three come and show us how in the world's south and east one studies the stars. All of us highly educated northern astronomers can only marvel at what they show us. "Have you realized at all," they ask — very politely and modestly, not in a know-all attitude — "have you realized at all that the halls you work in are closed above and on the sides? And that they are extremely well lit: with flashes of inspiration and fireworks of ideas and, in general, lots of neon light? Spotlights are turned on, showers of flashing lights come down, advertising signs are put up, screens are put up, and so on. You also have expensive electrical devices that can most certainly be helpful, but — well, yes: closed up there, and on the sides, and in addition to that everything is brightly lit up: under these circumstances discoveries in the starry sky can hardly be expected!"

We are a little embarrassed. "How do *you* do it then? How would *you* go about studying the stars?" "Well, we take our equipment (much more modest and often operated without electricity) out of our research halls (which are much lower and more impoverished than yours), *and bring it outside:* into the open, into the streets, to the people in the cities, even into the slums, into the villages, to all unholy and holy places, and we even take it to the observation sites of other proveniences (Buddhist, or Native Indian, or African places that were long thought of as not being noble enough). We ask the people we encounter what *they* see. And we try to provide them with equipment that *they* can handle. We neither do it all by ourselves, nor do we explicitly show them how to do it, but we observe these ordinary people, we use *their* tools, and — above all: we are out there in the open and *look up* together. And, believe us, there *are* stars out there!"

"Yes, yes," we agree, "there are stars. That much we know. We know that from ancient scripts, and songs, and poems. But all of these stars are so old. We need something with a new glimmer. And you: don't you need something very much different than star sightings, if you are really honest? Don't you, don't your people, desperately need the bare essentials for living? Don't you need, above all, economical and technical development, that is, a basic northern standard?" "That is true" is the answer. "We do search for that together with them and for them, and together with them we do fight for its realization, not the way you are doing it in your countries, but in a way that is suitable for us. But, curiously enough, the starry sky itself, in all its wide variety and glimmering beauty, helps one to find. It encourages one to seek, it gives light while searching, it shows the direction for the search."

Funny. The situation with the "Astronomers from the East" was somehow similar. They, too, came from far away, from parts of the world that were less in the center of interest; most probably, they had the wrong astronomical background knowledge, wrong basic convictions, and questionable equipment. But in the end, they were at the right place. And they let the whole world know what they had seen.

necessary—will always result in improved circumstances.

In recent years, countless numbers of books have been published in which the authors have extolled the idea of abundance—"The universe is a manifestation of God's creative power and you can have as much of its resources as you want if you will learn how be in harmonious relationship with it." While it is true that the universe can provide for all of our needs, it is not spiritually useful to cultivate an arrogant attitude of acquisitiveness characterized by aggression, greed, and compulsive endeavors to grasp, possess, and control. It is more beneficial, and soul-satisfying, to determine what our major purposes in life are, and learn how to be sufficiently prosperous in every way so that they can be successfully accomplished.

Very few readers of books with prosperity themes experience long-term benefits. The causes vary. They may not be able to comprehend the message. They may be unable to change their point of view from conditioned, personality-centered self-conscious states to awareness of themselves as Self- (soul) determined spiritual beings. They may be easily distracted from their goals. Or, they may be complacently satisfied with their prevailing mental attitudes and thought processes, addictive behaviors, familiar circumstances, and acquired relationships.

We have a prosperity consciousness when we are undeniably aware of wholeness, of *having*. Endeavors to manifest the effects of a prosperity consciousness— mental, emotional, and physical health, intellectual discernment, creativity, orderly circumstances, supportive relationships, timely events, and abundant resources— without vivid awareness of the wholeness of life will always either fall short of the goal or fail to produce permanent results. Why is this so? Because we cannot experience or manifest that which is not already in our consciousness.

When awareness of wholeness, of *having*, is our normal state, its effects are naturally expressive. States of consciousness and mental states produce effects after their own kind in accord with the natural, therefore reliable and predictable, principles of causation. Our personal experiences, behaviors, and circumstances always perfectly correspond with our habitual, subjective states of consciousness, mental attitudes, dominant thoughts, and consciously known or subliminal desires.

Because states of consciousness and mental states can cause effects, every person—happy or unhappy, healthy or unhealthy, successful or not, rich or poor—is always consciously or unconsciously flawlessly self-determining their experiences and circumstances.

A healthy-minded, emotionally mature person who desires improved circumstances will respond favorably to opportunities to learn how to be self-reliant and to live more effectively. Some individuals, whose actions have been unproductive of desired results or who prefer to believe themselves to be victims of fate, karma, adverse planetary influences, genetic factors, economic or societal trends and circumstances, or the malicious thoughts or actions of others, may not want to be reminded that they are contributing to their suffering and misfortune. They may complain, asserting that God does not love them ... life isn't fair ... others are more fortunate ... no one understands or cares about them ... they are incapable of helping themselves because they are victims of circumstances beyond their control. The truth, when appre-